The Beader's
Colour Mixing Directory

The Beader's
Colour Mixing Directory

200 colour schemes for beautiful beadwork

SANDRA WALLACE

SEARCH
PRESS

A QUARTO BOOK

Published in 2007 by Search Press Ltd.
Wellwood, North Farm Road
Tunbridge Wells
Kent TN2 3DR
United Kingdom

Reprinted 2008

ISBN-10: 1-84448-215-4
ISBN-13: 978-1-84448-215-3

Conceived, designed and produced by
Quarto Publishing plc
The Old Brewery, 6 Blundell Street
London N7 9BH

QUAR.BDI

Project Editor Lindsay Kaubi
Art Editor Julie Joubinaux
Designer Michelle Canatella
Assistant Art Director Penny Cobb
Photographer Philip Wilkins
Copy Editor Claire Wedderburn-Maxwell
Illustrators Kuo Kang Chen and Jurgen Ziewe
Picture Researcher Claudia Tate
Proofreader Robert Harries
Indexer Helen Snaith

Art Director Moira Clinch
Publisher Paul Carslake

Colour separation by Modern Age Repro House Ltd., Hong Kong
Printed by SNP Leefung Printers Ltd., China

Note to the reader
While every care has been taken with the colour reproduction in
this book, the limitations of the printing process mean we cannot
guarantee total colour accuracy in every instance.

Contents

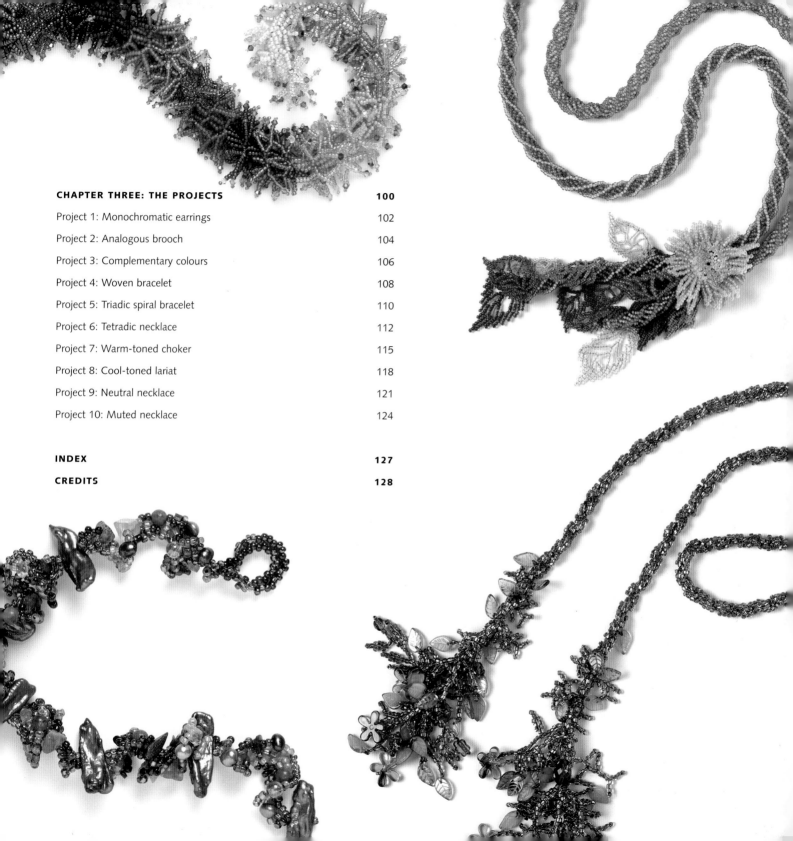

INTRODUCTION

Colour is an important aspect of our lives and often affects our emotions; we feel cheerful on a sunny day when colours are bright, but quite disheartened on a grey misty day in autumn. We even use the phrase, 'the colour has gone out of my life', to convey that we feel low.

Often we are attracted to certain colours. When we shop, our eyes are drawn to the colour of an item before we look at the texture or pattern. Most of us are blessed with an in-built sense of which colours go together, but sometimes we lack the confidence to experiment with new colour schemes. Beginners to beadwork can be daunted by the vast array of colours and finishes of beads available. It's not just a matter of which colour to put with which but also the proportions of each colour to use. Whether you are a novice beadworker or more experienced, this book will help you to develop your love of colour.

Colour is all around us and often we just need our eyes opened to its possibilities. I hope that my love of colour and texture is evident in this book and that this inspires you to be more adventurous too. You may even find yourself loving colour schemes that you previously would have avoided!

Sandra Wallace

About this book

The book is divided into three sections. The first section is an introduction to colour theory featuring core lessons on topics such as the colour wheel, tonal values and complementary colours. Knowledge of colour theory will save a lot of trial and error when it comes to choosing a colour scheme.

At the heart of the book is a stunning directory of beading colour schemes. This main section is organized into broad themes and sub-organized into colour 'stories'. The reader can browse the pages for an inspiring scheme for their next project, choosing from the vast and beautiful array of beadwork on display.

The final section of the book is a series of ten projects. The projects range from simple techniques for the beginner to more advanced projects for those with some experience. They utilize a variety of colour schemes and each has four alternative colour variations so that there is something for everyone.

Opposite page 127, you'll find a handy fold-out flap, which you can have open while you refer to the Colour Schemes and Projects pages. The flap provides an instant reference to the colour wheel and the main types of colour schemes introduced in the Colour Theory chapter.

HOW TO USE THE 'COLOUR RECIPES'

Each item in the directory of colour schemes is accompanied by a graphic 'colour recipe'. This device identifies the colours used and the proportions in which they are used. Each device comprises 20 coloured bars, each bar representing five percent of the beadwork piece. Each of these bars is coloured to indicate the proportion of each colour used. This neat device gives a detailed picture of the scheme and allows the beader to use the colourway in their own pieces.

Graphic device

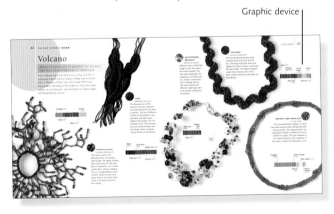

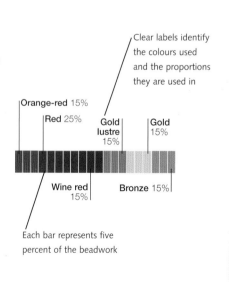

Clear labels identify the colours used and the proportions they are used in

Orange-red 15%

Red 25%

Gold lustre 15%

Gold 15%

Wine red 15%

Bronze 15%

Each bar represents five percent of the beadwork

chapter one
COLOUR THEORY

All the basic colour schemes are explained and demonstrated in this section with a variety of examples and clear diagrams, enabling the beadworker to understand how the schemes work and how to compose their own colour scheme in the same style. Applying the rules set out in this chapter to your own beadwork will ensure that you produce beautiful and harmonious pieces of jewellery.

The colour wheel

THE COLOUR WHEEL IS AT THE HEART OF COLOUR THEORY.

A colour wheel is a logical arrangement of pure hues. It is used to show how the primary colours relate to each other, and how mixing two or more colours together creates new colours. A colour wheel is helpful as a guide to mixing colours and is a valuable tool for beaders when devising new colour schemes.

Many variations of the colour wheel have been designed, and they all have their place. For instance, mixing light is different to mixing pigments, so different approaches are needed. Most colour wheels are a 'spectrum', with the ends joined together in a circle, so that the red and purple ends meet.

THE PIGMENT WHEEL

Painters and textile artists use the pigment wheel to mix paints and dyes. This wheel has three 'primary colours' of red (**1**), yellow (**5**), and blue (**9**). Mixing two adjacent primary colours produces the secondary colours: orange (**3**), green (**7**) and purple (**11**). Mixing a primary colour with an adjacent secondary colour forms a 'tertiary colour'. There are six tertiary colours (**2**, **4**, **6**, **8**, **10**, **12**). (See also page 12.)

Far more colours than these twelve are available to the beader because of the numerous finishes available in beads. Also, secondary and tertiary colours need not be straight purple or blue-green beads respectively; they could be fuchsia-lined blue (which gives the appearance of purple) or blue-lined green beads.

TONAL VALUE AND INTENSITY

Colours can be changed significantly by adding black, white, or other colours to the pure hue. This means they can be lightened, darkened or dulled. By mixing all three primary colours, black and white in differing proportions, you will create a variety of browns or black and the neutral shades. It is also worth noting that light reflected off adjacent beads will alter the bead colour. When placed next to other beads, transparent beads can often 'lose' their colour, particularly if they are pastel-coloured. (See also page 14.)

Red (1)

Yellow (5)

Blue (9)

Orange (3)

Purple (11)

Green (7)

Yellow-green (6)

Red-orange (2)

Yellow-orange (4)

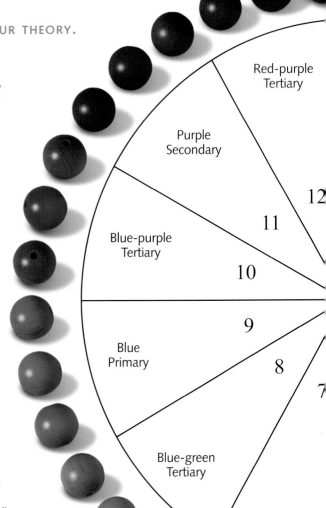

Red-purple
Tertiary

Purple
Secondary

Blue-purple
Tertiary

Blue
Primary

Blue-green
Tertiary

Green
Secondary

12

11

10

9

8

7

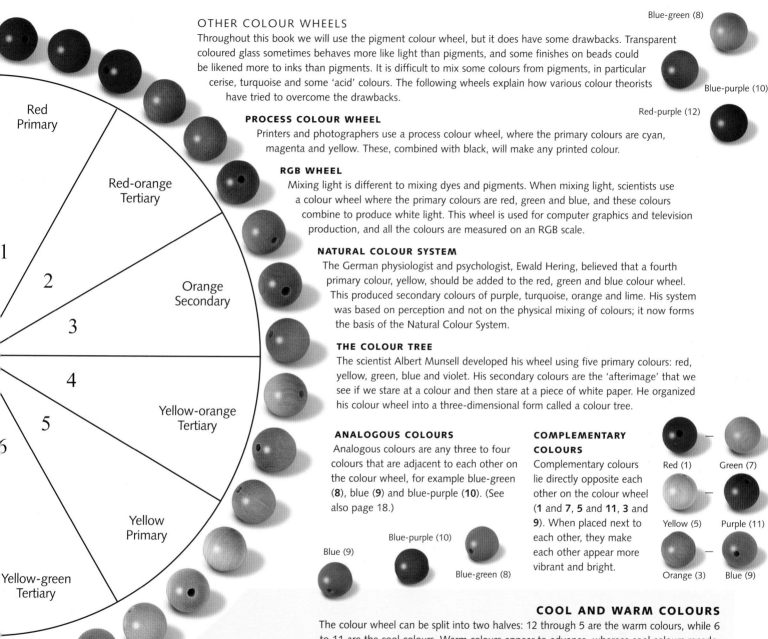

Blue-green (8)

Blue-purple (10)

Red-purple (12)

OTHER COLOUR WHEELS

Throughout this book we will use the pigment colour wheel, but it does have some drawbacks. Transparent coloured glass sometimes behaves more like light than pigments, and some finishes on beads could be likened more to inks than pigments. It is difficult to mix some colours from pigments, in particular cerise, turquoise and some 'acid' colours. The following wheels explain how various colour theorists have tried to overcome the drawbacks.

PROCESS COLOUR WHEEL

Printers and photographers use a process colour wheel, where the primary colours are cyan, magenta and yellow. These, combined with black, will make any printed colour.

RGB WHEEL

Mixing light is different to mixing dyes and pigments. When mixing light, scientists use a colour wheel where the primary colours are red, green and blue, and these colours combine to produce white light. This wheel is used for computer graphics and television production, and all the colours are measured on an RGB scale.

NATURAL COLOUR SYSTEM

The German physiologist and psychologist, Ewald Hering, believed that a fourth primary colour, yellow, should be added to the red, green and blue colour wheel. This produced secondary colours of purple, turquoise, orange and lime. His system was based on perception and not on the physical mixing of colours; it now forms the basis of the Natural Colour System.

THE COLOUR TREE

The scientist Albert Munsell developed his wheel using five primary colours: red, yellow, green, blue and violet. His secondary colours are the 'afterimage' that we see if we stare at a colour and then stare at a piece of white paper. He organized his colour wheel into a three-dimensional form called a colour tree.

ANALOGOUS COLOURS

Analogous colours are any three to four colours that are adjacent to each other on the colour wheel, for example blue-green (**8**), blue (**9**) and blue-purple (**10**). (See also page 18.)

Blue (9)

Blue-purple (10)

Blue-green (8)

COMPLEMENTARY COLOURS

Complementary colours lie directly opposite each other on the colour wheel (**1** and **7**, **5** and **11**, **3** and **9**). When placed next to each other, they make each other appear more vibrant and bright.

Red (1) — Green (7)

Yellow (5) — Purple (11)

Orange (3) — Blue (9)

Labels on colour wheel (left):
Red Primary
Red-orange Tertiary
Orange Secondary
Yellow-orange Tertiary
Yellow Primary
Yellow-green Tertiary
1 2 3 4 5 6

COOL AND WARM COLOURS

The colour wheel can be split into two halves: 12 through 5 are the warm colours, while 6 to 11 are the cool colours. Warm colours appear to advance, whereas cool colours recede. This can make the warm colours appear more dominant in a design that uses equal amounts of both. In this respect, compared to other crafters, beaders have a great advantage because they can use a gold-lined blue bead, for example. The gold will warm up the blue and it can be used with warm colours, where the blue on its own wouldn't work. (See also page 16.)

Primary, secondary and tertiary colours

THE TWELVE COLOURS OF THE PIGMENT WHEEL SPECTRUM.

The pigment wheel has three primary colours: red, yellow and blue. You cannot make these colours by mixing any other colour. However, mixing these colours together in various proportions produces every other colour on the wheel.

Blue-purple

Red-purple

Yellow

Wooden: Orange

Glass: Green

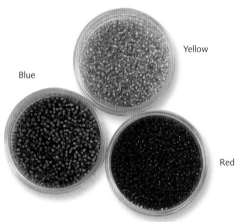

Blue

SECONDARY COLOURS: SHAPE, SIZE AND MATERIALS

Simple designs in secondary colours can be made more interesting and unusual by combining beads of different shapes, sizes and materials. These three groups – orange wooden beads, green glass and purple matt amethyst – could form a strong focal point in a design, providing contrasts of colour and surface texture.

Red

Amethyst: Purple

PRIMARY COLOURS: SHAPE, SIZE AND MATERIALS

The appearance of primary colours varies depending on the material from which the beads are made. Yellow wooden beads are opaque, and reflect very little light, so are the same colour all over. Red plastic beads are translucent so that the 'local' (actual) colour is modified by the paler cores within. Ridges on the blue glass beads create strong highlights and shadows, so that less local colour is evident.

Wooden: Yellow

SECONDARY COLOURS

Mixing two adjacent primary colours together produces a secondary colour. The secondary colours are orange, green and purple.

Orange

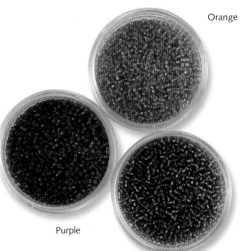

Plastic: Red

Glass: Blue

Purple

Green

Yellow-orange

Red-orange

Blue-green

Yellow-green

TERTIARY COLOURS

Mixing a primary colour with an adjacent secondary colour creates a tertiary colour. There are six tertiary colours: red-orange, yellow-orange, yellow-green, blue-green, blue-purple and red-purple.

USING SECONDARY AND TERTIARY COLOURS

In beadwork, there are many ways of producing these colours. Beaders could use a colour-lined bead or a coloured thread to give the appearance of a secondary or tertiary colour. For example, a blue glass bead lined with fuchsia would give the appearance of a purple bead. Some of the richer shades of purple are often difficult to obtain in glass, so purple beads are often coated or lined. A coloured thread or wire can alter the appearance of a transparent bead, especially if it is a pale colour, while a blue thread used with green beads would make the beadwork appear blue-green. (See also pages 28–31.)

It is worth noting that when you place one colour next to another, your perception of the original colour will change. If you want a bead to look lighter then place darker beads next to it. If you want it to appear brighter, place it amid duller beads.

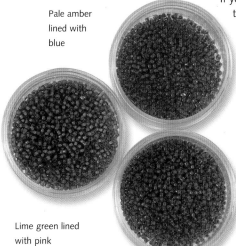

Pale amber lined with blue

Blue lined with fuchsia

Lime green lined with pink

TERTIARY COLOURS: SHAPE, SIZE, AND FINISH

The beadworker has a vast choice of shapes, sizes, and finishes in the tertiary colour range, and the groups shown here illustrate just a small selection. You could contrast dyed wooden beads in blues and purples with plastic beads in yellows and oranges, perhaps using faceted plastic beads or simulated amber for textural interest.

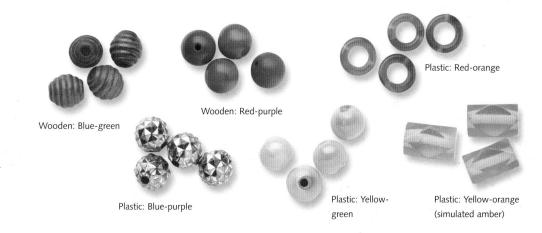

Wooden: Red-purple

Plastic: Red-orange

Wooden: Blue-green

Plastic: Blue-purple

Plastic: Yellow-green

Plastic: Yellow-orange (simulated amber)

Tonal values, tints and shades

ALWAYS CONSIDER THE TONAL VALUE OF THE BEAD, AS WELL AS THE COLOUR.

Tonal value refers to the lightness and darkness of a colour. We can change the tone of a colour by adding white, black or grey. A tint is a colour that has been lightened by adding white, while a shade is a colour that has been darkened by adding black.

TONAL VALUE
When choosing colours it is important to consider the tonal value, as the placement of light and dark beads can have a dramatic effect on the finished piece. Lemon yellow has a very light tonal value, appearing almost white, while indigo has the darkest tonal value, appearing almost black.

Both red and green have the same tonal value, so in a black and white photo they appear the same colour grey.

It is sometimes difficult to judge tonal values in a piece of beadwork or a collection of beads. The eye looks at the colour first, and doesn't immediately consider the tonal value. The best way to comprehend this is to imagine taking a black-and-white photograph of the beads. Which beads would be the palest grey, and which the darkest grey? Are they all the same tone, i.e. would they all come out as mid-grey in the photograph? Red and grass green are very different colours, but they share the same tonal value, so they would both appear tonally as mid-grey.

TONE IN JEWELLERY
Beadwork that is all the same tonal value could look bland and dull, especially if the same finish was used for all the beads. Dark-coloured matt beads have the darkest tonal value while pale-coloured transparent beads have the lightest tonal value.

Pale transparent blue beads   Dark matt navy beads

CREATING TONAL INTEREST
Jewellery that has no variation in tone need not look dull if you select a variety of beads. If you used pearl, transparent and matt beads in a pair of earrings then you would ensure there is a difference in the appearance of the tone. This is because of the way that the different beads reflect or absorb the light.

TONAL CHANGES

Adding white or black to a pure hue changes the tone of a colour and sometimes changes the colour. For example, adding black to yellow will give lime or olive green, rather than dark yellow. Below are some examples of how colour and tone can change with the proportions of white and black they contain.

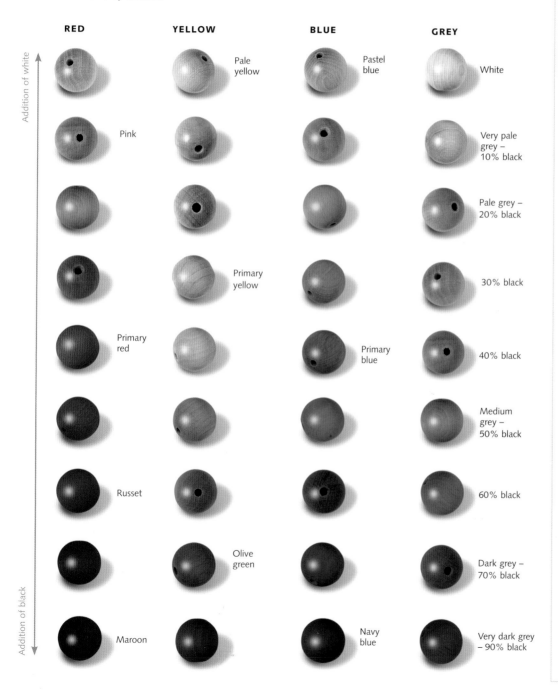

RED   YELLOW   BLUE   GREY

Addition of white →

RED column:
Pink
Primary red
Russet
Maroon

YELLOW column:
Pale yellow
Primary yellow
Olive green

BLUE column:
Pastel blue
Primary blue
Navy blue

GREY column:
White
Very pale grey – 10% black
Pale grey – 20% black
30% black
40% black
Medium grey – 50% black
60% black
Dark grey – 70% black
Very dark grey – 90% black

Addition of black ↓

INTENSITY OR SATURATION

This is a measure of how bright or dull a colour is. A colour can be neutralized by adding its complementary colour; for example, if you add purple to yellow, it will dull the yellow. The more purple that is added the more the yellow is neutralized, eventually becoming almost black. Adding purple to yellow would produce the colours shown below. This shows the range in intensity that you can produce:

Yellow

Khaki

Very dark olive green

Addition of purple to yellow →

Warm and cool colours

RED HOT OR ICE COLD, ALWAYS CONSIDER THE WARMTH OF THE COLOURS USED.

The colour wheel can be divided into two halves: **warm colours** – red, orange and yellow; and **cool colours** – green, blue and purple. Combining warm and cool colours in your beadwork can create very interesting effects.

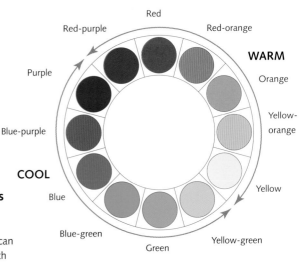

COOL COLOURS

Cool colours are restful and calm, like the blues and greens seen in nature. The addition of a warm colour to a cool colour scheme will prevent it from being too cold and clinical. Cool colours appear smaller and have a tendency to recede. Because of this, they work well as background colours as they rarely draw attention to themselves.

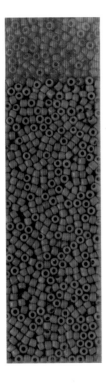

WARM COLOURS

Warm colours are vivid, bold and exciting, but they can be toned down with the use of cool colours or by using tints. Warm colours appear larger and have a tendency to advance. Beaders need to be careful that, when using warm colours in a colour scheme, they don't overwhelm a design. Think about using a warm colour if you would like to draw attention to one element of a design, as in complementary colour schemes (see page 20).

HOW IT WORKS

The colour wheel is split into two halves: warm hues and cool hues. A piece of jewellery made from all warm or all cool colours would be naturally harmonious.

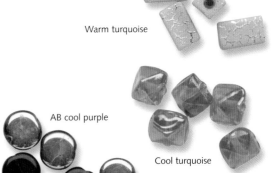

Warm turquoise

AB cool purple

Cool turquoise

WARM AND COOL IN ONE COLOUR

The rectangular turquoise and silver beads are warmer as they are more yellow-toned than the faceted square beads, which are bluer. The same is true for purple, which can be red-toned or blue-toned. Compare the Chinese knot beads to the glass beads.

Warm purple

Monochromatic colour schemes

A SINGLE COLOUR CAN BE INTERESTING IF THE TONE OR FINISH IS VARIED.

Monochromatic colour schemes consist of one colour that is either changed in tonal value or in intensity (see page 15). Yellow, for instance, could range from palest yellow through khaki to almost black in intensity, and from the brightest yellow through to lime and olive green to almost black in tonal value.

DIFFERENT FINISHES

For beadworkers, a monochromatic colour scheme need not mean using different coloured beads from light to dark. A monochromatic scheme could consist of beads that are all the same colour but have different finishes, for example opaque beads, matt beads, lustred beads, lined crystal beads and transparent beads. Even if these are all the same colour, in a piece of beadwork they would all reflect the light differently so there would be a noticeable difference in tone between the beads.

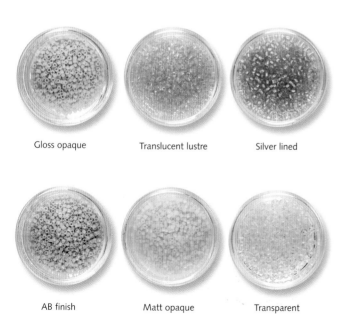

Gloss opaque   Translucent lustre   Silver lined

AB finish   Matt opaque   Transparent

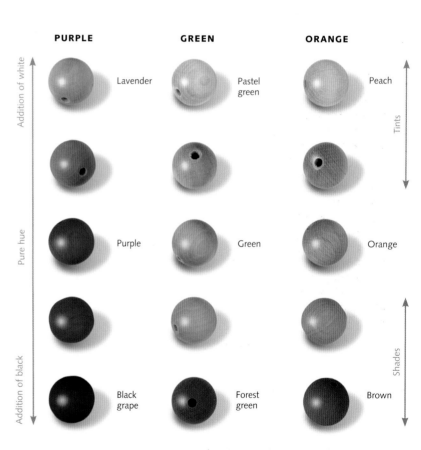

PURPLE   GREEN   ORANGE

Addition of white — Lavender, Pastel green, Peach (Tints)

Pure hue — Purple, Green, Orange

Addition of black — Black grape, Forest green, Brown (Shades)

TONAL CHANGES

These rows of beads show how secondary colours can be changed by adding an increasing amount of white or black to the pure hues. These different tones, tints and shades can then be used to create monochromatic colour schemes.

Analogous colour schemes

THESE HARMONIOUS COLOURS HAVE A WONDERFULLY MELLOW EFFECT.

Analogous colours are any three to four colours that are adjacent to each other on the colour wheel, for example orange, orange-yellow, yellow and yellow-green are analogous. Analogous colour schemes are very harmonious because they usually have a common colour linking at least three of the colours, in the case of this example, yellow.

ANALOGOUS COLOURS

Analogous schemes are more interesting than monochromatic colour schemes because they have a broader range of colours, but they are still quite easy schemes to put together. These colour schemes usually lean towards either a warm or a cool palette. Think of a woodland forest in autumn with its tints and shades ranging from a variety of greens through gold and rust to brown.

USING ANALOGOUS SCHEMES

In beadwork, a colour can be changed significantly by giving it an Aurora Borealis (AB) coating (see page 29), or by lining the bead with a different colour. Therefore, analogous colours could include different finishes or types of beads, as well as different coloured beads.

Colour scheme: Red-purple, purple, blue-purple, blue

Colour scheme: Tints of yellow-orange, orange, red

Colour scheme: Blue, blue-green, green, yellow-green

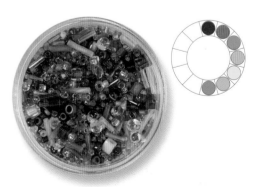

Colour scheme: Green, yellow-green, yellow, yellow-orange, orange, red-orange, red

FOUR ANALOGOUS COLOUR SCHEMES

Below are some examples of analogous colour schemes. Warm colour schemes are those containing red, orange and yellow, and cool schemes contain blues and greens. Combinations of tints and shades can be used in addition to the variations illustrated on this page.

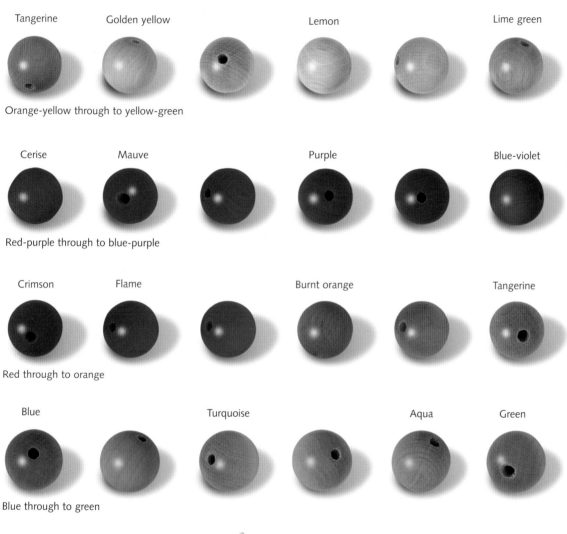

Tangerine   Golden yellow   Lemon   Lime green

Orange-yellow through to yellow-green

Cerise   Mauve   Purple   Blue-violet

Red-purple through to blue-purple

Crimson   Flame   Burnt orange   Tangerine

Red through to orange

Blue   Turquoise   Aqua   Green

Blue through to green

ANALOGOUS FRINGED CUFF

This cuff is made from seed beads in red and pale mauve, with just a touch of clashing blue on the tips of the fringes. This bold use of a broad range of analogous hues makes this scheme slightly clashing.

Complementary colour schemes

IDEAL FOR VIBRANT, HIGHLY CONTRASTING BEADWORK.

Complementary colours lie directly opposite each other on the colour wheel. They are either a primary colour with its opposite secondary colour, such as purple and yellow, or two opposing tertiary colours, such as yellow-green and red-purple. A complementary colour will bring out the colours of the other beads.

Complementary colour schemes are always interesting, because when complementary colours are placed next to each other they make each other appear more vibrant and bright. A complementary colour scheme can be very harmonious if the correct proportions of each colour are used. Think of a holly tree with berries, or purple irises. Nature has a way of using complementary colours in the right proportions in a colour scheme.

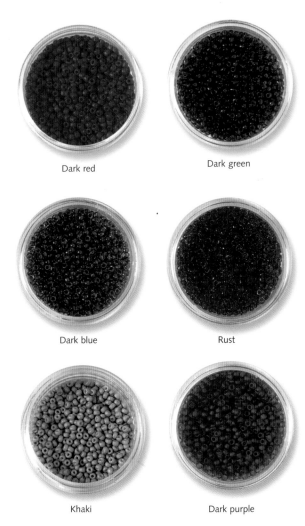

Dark red   Dark green

Dark blue   Rust

Khaki   Dark purple

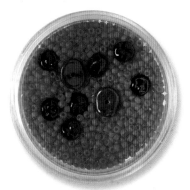

Uncomfortable and overwhelming: orange with blue accent beads

Striking but pleasing: blue with orange accent beads

GETTING PROPORTIONS RIGHT

Using colour in harmonious proportions is important when using a complementary colour scheme. A scheme where the warmer colour occupies a smaller area than the cooler colour is much more pleasing to the eye than vice versa. For example, a necklace in shades of mid- to dark blue would be beautiful but classic. Consider the same necklace with a few accent beads in orange – this necklace would be striking and attention-grabbing. However, not many people would want to wear a bright orange necklace with a few blue accent beads.

COMPLEMENTARY SHADES

These colours are shades of the primary and secondary colours, i.e. they have black added to them. Shades of the complementary colours yellow and purple would be the more muted tones of khaki and dark purple. This would make for a very subtle complementary colour scheme.

SPLIT COMPLEMENTARY COLOUR SCHEMES

Split complementary colour schemes use any colour together with the two colours either side of its complementary colour, for instance red with blue-green and yellow-green, or yellow-orange together with blue and purple. Either the colour or its two complementary colours should dominate in this scheme, as equal proportions of each colour could jar.

Colour scheme: Yellow-orange, purple, blue

Colour scheme: Red, blue-green, yellow-green

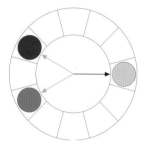

HOW IT WORKS

Yellow-orange is the main colour. Its complementary colour is blue-purple, and the split complementary colours are blue and purple.

Colour scheme: Blue, red-orange, yellow-orange

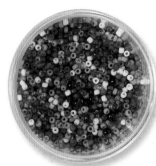 

Colour scheme: Red-purple, yellow, green

Pale pink

Pale blue

Lemon

COMPLEMENTARY TINTS

White added to the primary and secondary colours would give the tints shown here. Lavender and lemon would give a very delicate colour scheme for summer. Complementary schemes do not have to be either tints or shades but can be a combination of tints and shades. This would give more variation within the colour scheme.

Pale green

Peach

Lavender

Triadic and tetradic colour schemes

FOR STRIKING JEWELLERY, THESE SCHEMES OFFER GREAT VARIETY.

A **triadic colour** scheme uses three colours that are **equally** spaced around the colour wheel. A tetradic colour scheme is made up of a total of four colours: two colours that are not adjacent to each other on the wheel, together with their complementary opposites.

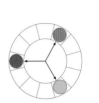

Colour scheme: Red, yellow, blue

TRIADIC COLOUR SCHEMES

A triadic colour scheme uses three evenly spaced colours. These could be the three primary colours, three secondary colours or three of the tertiary colours. These schemes offer a strong contrast, but they are more balanced and not as highly contrasting as the complementary scheme (see page 20).

The proportions of the three colours is very important. If the colours have a tendency to clash, then it is best to tone them down. One colour should dominate, while the third colour is often used just as an accent colour. Consider a bracelet design of rich purple flowers with orange centres and a green background.

Colour scheme: Red-orange, blue-purple, yellow-green

Colour scheme: Green, purple, orange

Glass: blue lined ridges

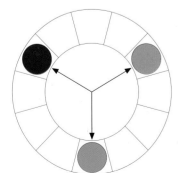

HOW IT WORKS
Triadic colour schemes consist of three colours spaced evenly on the colour wheel.
Triadic colour schemes include:
• Red, yellow, and blue
• Red-orange, blue-purple and yellow-green
• Green, purple and orange (shown here)

Glass: yellow twisted drops

Glass: red faceted oval

TEXTURAL VARIETY
Beaders are not confined to using just seed beads in triadic schemes. Shaped glass beads could be used as accent beads; the different shapes add textural variety and balance the whole design.

TETRADIC COLOUR SCHEMES

A tetradic colour scheme, also called a double complementary scheme, is similar to the split complementary scheme (see page 21), but it uses two colours from each side of the colour wheel. This scheme gives more variety than any other colour scheme, but it is also the most difficult to balance. As with the triadic scheme, it is best for one colour to dominate and the others to be used in lesser amounts. Imagine a necklace in one of the stunning colour schemes listed below. This is not for the fainthearted, but would definitely suit those who love colour.

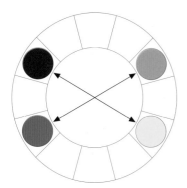

HOW IT WORKS

Tetradic colour schemes consist of two colours from either side of the colour wheel: two sets of complementary colours. Tetradic colour schemes include:
- Purple, blue, orange, and yellow (shown here)
- Green, blue, red, and orange
- Yellow-orange, yellow-green, blue-purple, and red-purple
- Red-orange, red-purple, blue-green, and yellow-green

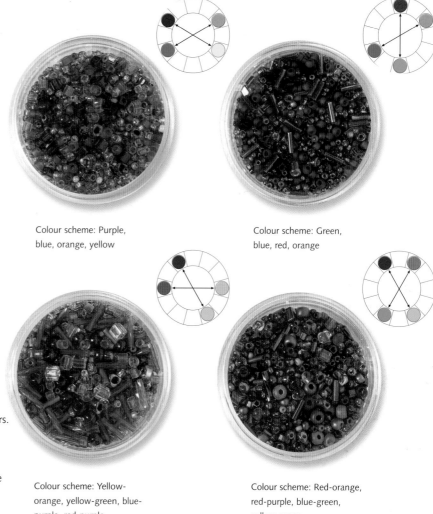

Colour scheme: Purple, blue, orange, yellow

Colour scheme: Green, blue, red, orange

Colour scheme: Yellow-orange, yellow-green, blue-purple, red-purple

Colour scheme: Red-orange, red-purple, blue-green, yellow-green

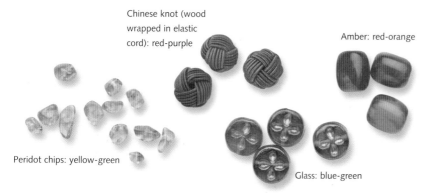

Chinese knot (wood wrapped in elastic cord): red-purple

Amber: red-orange

Peridot chips: yellow-green

Glass: blue-green

FEATURE BEADS AND ACCENT BEADS IN TETRADIC SCHEMES

The proportions of the colours used in a tetradic scheme can sometimes be difficult to balance. Beads such as the red-orange barrel amber or the blue-green glass shown here would be ideal as accent beads in a tetradic scheme. Seed bead necklaces could be given an extra feature by adding the yellow-green peridot for texture or the red-purple Chinese knots for a difference in materials.

Neutral colour schemes

NEUTRALS WORK WELL WITH ALL THE COLOURS ON THE COLOUR WHEEL.

Neutral colours do not appear on the colour wheel but instead are formed by mixing the three primary colours in differing proportions to obtain shades of brown. These browns include **grey-brown** (donkey brown), **warm red-brown** (chestnut) and **yellow-brown** (dark khaki brown).

White, black and grey aren't strictly neutral colours, but are often treated as such.

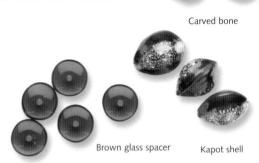

Carved bone

Brown glass spacer   Kapot shell

COLOUR, TEXTURE AND DECORATION
When using neutral colours, look especially for beads with interesting shapes, textures, or decoration. You'll also find that there are many neutral coloured beads made from natural materials. The examples shown here are glass spacers in muted brown, carved and decorated bone, and beads made from varnished kapot shell.

Gloss-cream   Yellow-beige   Matt-cream

Ridged horn ovals

Glass faceted drops

Smoky quartz

Pink-beige   Grey-beige

WHITE-BASED NEUTRAL COLOURS
If white is added to the browns then you get a range of off-whites, cream, taupe and beige. Neutral colours are low-saturation colours; they have come from a mixture of primary colours so they are not bright or intense.

Cool grey: Pale grey

Warm grey: AB transparent

Cool grey: Dark grey

Glass lined with silver foil

Haematite

GREY NEUTRALS

Greys that have come from a mixture of the primary colours are mostly warm greys. The grey that is made by mixing black and white and not the colours on the colour wheel is not exactly a neutral. However, when thinking of colour we do treat grey as a neutral. The greys that have come from a mixture of black and white are cool greys.

Warm grey: Matt opaque

BLACK, WHITE AND BROWN

Beads that are basically black and white can look extremely sophisticated, especially if they have a shiny, light-reflecting surface, while browns can be given the appearance of semi-precious stones. Beads made from actual semi-precious stones are available, but most are also imitated in glass.

Leopard-skin jasper

Warm: Red-brown

Warm: Yellow-brown

Cool: Grey-brown

Cool: Metallic grey-brown

WARM AND COOL NEUTRALS

Neutral colours can be warm or cool depending on the proportions of the three primary colours. Warm neutrals have a greater proportion of red and yellow, while cool neutrals have a greater proportion of blue.

Muted colour schemes

FOR SUBTLE – BUT ATTRACTIVE – BEADWORK, EXPERIMENT WITH MUTED COLOURS.

Muted or greyed colour schemes are classic and understated. They don't shout for attention but prefer to fade into the background. Using muted colours in the basic colour schemes, such as analogous schemes (see page 18) and complementary schemes (see page 20), gives another dimension to composing colour schemes.

MAKING MUTED COLOURS

Mixing a hue with its complementary colour or grey makes tones of a colour. For example, if grey is added to the complementary colours of yellow-green and red-purple then you get sage green and muted mauve respectively.

MUTED COLOURS IN JEWELLERY

The lower-intensity muted colours are easy to use together. Imagine a necklace in 'earth' colours made from ochre, beige and rust beads, enriched with grey-blue and slate. This analogous colour scheme with the complementary blue always looks good.

SAMPLE BEAD MIXES FOR MUTED COLOUR SCHEMES

Moss green, dusty rose, off-white

Slate blue, grey, lavender, mauve, dull gold

Lavender and pale khaki

Slate blue, grey, white

Russet, pink, off-white, caramel

SAMPLE MUTED COLOUR SCHEMES

Dark blue and dark amber

Terracotta, teal, warm beige, cream

Olive green, brown, dark mustard, beige

Navy, purple, pink, amber

Black and white

BLACK AND WHITE BEADS CAN BE USED TO STRIKING EFFECT.

Black and white do not appear on the colour wheel, but when combined with other colours they produce tints and shades of the original colour. When you mix black and white together in various proportions they form a neutral grey, with shades ranging from pale grey to charcoal.

BLACK AND WHITE IN JEWELLERY

In beadwork, you can use virtually any proportion of black and white beads together. A necklace would look very chic if half black and half white were used, but would look no less stylish if either black or white were dominant. Warm colours appear more brilliant against black and are somewhat duller against white. The same size red bead would look larger surrounded by black beads than white.

Turquoise and white

White and red

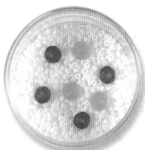

White, blue and green

WHITE

White drains colours such as red and orange, but blues and greens look wonderful set against white. There is a purity with white that enhances the cool colours perfectly. Icy pale blue and crystal white beads look fantastic together, like drifts of clean snow, but for a warmer feel try using turquoise with white.

Black and red

Black and purple

BLACK

Next to black, warm, pure colours advance more than muted or cooler colours. A necklace made with black beads and red accent beads would look stunning, the red looking very dramatic. The same black necklace with purple accent beads would look more sophisticated. Shades harmonize well with black producing an elegant piece of jewellery, but sometimes tints look insipid.

Black and tints

Black and shades

BLACK AND WHITE BEADS

Black and white have been used in equal proportions in these beads. They could be strung in a necklace with small white beads, small black beads or a combination of the two to great effect.

Different types of beads

SURFACE FINISH IS VERY IMPORTANT TO A BEADWORKER.

The texture of a surface influences the colour – the rougher a surface is, the darker it will appear. Matt beads absorb the light that falls on them, so they will appear darker, while shiny beads will reflect more light and appear lighter. It can be a real asset to use different finishes in a necklace, but it can create an eyesore if a certain finish is used in the wrong place.

It is always a good idea for novice beadworkers to stitch a small sample using the project beads. This ensures that the colours and finishes work in harmony together.

COLOURFASTNESS
Some finishes of beads and colour-lined beads are not colourfast, especially reds, pinks and purples. You can test for colourfastness by placing a dish of beads in a sunny window to see if they fade, or by adding bleach or acetone to the beads.

BEADS THAT APPEAR TO ADVANCE OR RECEDE
Shiny beads are very reflective and they pick up and mirror the colour from their surroundings – this is especially true for silver-lined beads. As a general rule, opaque colours and beads with shiny surface finishes appear to come forwards in a design. Transparent and 'greasy' colours or matt surface finishes tend to recede.

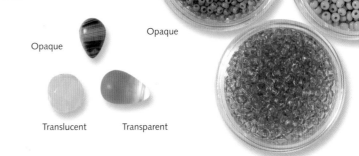

Transparent

Opaque

Opaque

Transparent

Transparent

Opaque

Translucent

Transparent

Clear transparent
lined with gold

Blue lined with fuchsia

LINED GLASS BEADS
Silver-lined glass beads are very bright and are best used sparingly unless you want to attract attention to yourself. Gold-lined beads can add warmth to a piece especially if the beads are made from transparent coloured glass. Colour-lined glass beads have an opaque colour inside a clear or coloured transparent bead. A white lining can show up the colour of a transparent glass bead without altering the colour greatly.

Transparent gold lined
with blue-green

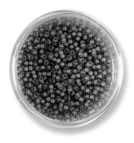

Clear transparent lined
with pink

Amber lined with grey

Opaque AB-coated

TRANSPARENT, TRANSLUCENT AND OPAQUE GLASS BEADS

Transparent beads allow light to pass through them, so if they are very pale they will 'lose' their colour in a necklace unless placed against skin or a white background. Translucent glass beads transmit light but you can't see through them, so they are sometimes called 'greasy' beads. Opaque beads do not allow the light to pass through them and they are often very bold in a design. An opaque or translucent orange bead would have a totally different effect in a piece of beadwork compared with a transparent orange bead.

Matt finish

Satin finish

Matt translucent, gold-lined

Matt translucent

Opaque lustre

Ceylon pearl

Opaque

Ceylon pearl

Ceylon pearl

MATT AND SATIN BEADS

Matt beads are opaque or transparent beads that have been etched to produce a non-reflective finish. They absorb the light so will appear darker than other beads even if they are the same colour. These beads recede into the background when placed with beads of other finishes. Satin beads are easy to use in beadwork, as they blend well with matt or shiny beads. They tend to come forwards in a design.

Gold lustre

LUSTRE

Opaque lustre beads are like pearls, and translucent lustre beads are called Ceylon beads. Some beads have a gold lustre coating, which shines when the light falls on it in a certain way.

Bronze metallic

Gold metallic AB-coated

Transparent AB-coated

AURORA BOREALIS (AB) COATING

This is a rainbow coating that is added to beads. It adds subtle variations of colour and gives added variation and depth to beadwork. This finish is sometimes called 'iris'.

Silver

Gunmetal

METAL, METAL-FINISH AND METALLIC BEADS

Glass seed beads can be coated with a metallic or metal finish in silver, gold, bronze or nickel. Pure silver and gold beads add a touch of luxury to a piece of jewellery. If a less glitzy effect is desired then you could use satin finish instead of gloss.

Transparent AB-coated

Other influences

BEAD SIZE AND SHAPE HAS AN IMPACT ON THE DESIGN.

As well as the colour, tone and finish of your beads, you need to consider the size and shape of the beads you want to use for your project. You also will need to think about the thread you wish to use, as well as the findings, as all these factors can make a difference to the end result.

SIZE OF BEAD

The size of bead is very important in a design. The most popular sizes of seed beads range from size 6 to size 15; the higher the number the smaller the bead. However, there are larger and smaller seed beads available.

Size 15 seed beads will give a much more dainty effect than a size 6. It is also possible to achieve more detail in a design if a smaller bead is used.

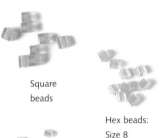

Bugle beads

Square beads

Hex beads: Size 8

Magatamas

Hex beads: Size 11

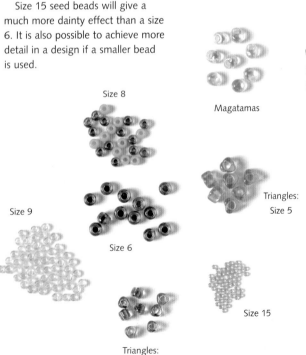

Size 8

Size 9

Size 6

Size 15

Triangles: Size 10

Triangles: Size 5

DIFFERENT SHAPES

Smaller beads come in a variety of shapes, including triangles, squares, bugle beads and seed beads. Some beads also have a different cut such as Charlottes and two-cut beads. There are also cylinder beads, hexagonal beads and twisted bugles to add even more variety. Wonderful sculptural and freeform bracelets, necklaces and pieces of beadwork can be made using these alone.

Yellow turquoise

Foil-lined Venetian

Abalone

Lampwork

Lampwork

Lampwork

FOCAL BEADS

Focal beads can range from semi-precious stones, shells and found objects to magnificent lampwork glass beads made by artists. You can use them as a starting point for a colour scheme or to add variety and texture. Used like this they merge into the overall scheme, becoming an integral part of the necklace. On the other hand, they can be the main focus of attention and the rest of the beadwork is there to complement them.

THREAD

The thread colour that you use is very important in your beadwork. There are so many colours of beading thread that it is usually possible to find a very good match to the colour of your beads. Of course, you may wish to make a feature of your thread and choose a contrasting colour, especially if you are using transparent beads. If there are a few colours in your design, or the colours are contrasting, then choose a thread that will work with most of the colours. Alternatively, use a grey or beige thread, as you will find that these threads will blend with most colours.

If the holes are large enough, you could thread beads on to a coloured cord, ribbon, leather thong or braided threads. These could be toning or contrasting and could be quite textural.

Coloured beading wires

Suede thong

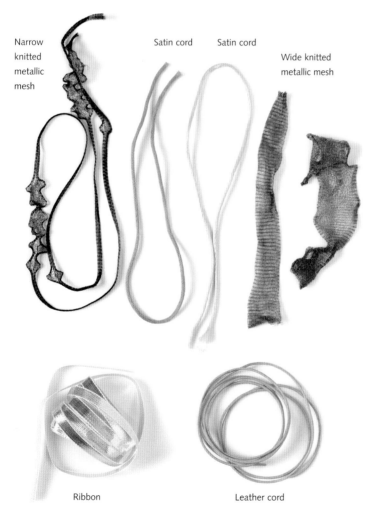

Narrow knitted metallic mesh

Satin cord

Satin cord

Wide knitted metallic mesh

Ribbon

Leather cord

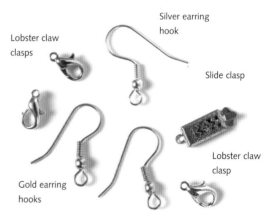

Lobster claw clasps

Silver earring hook

Slide clasp

Lobster claw clasp

Gold earring hooks

WIRE AND FINDINGS

Findings are the clasps, earring hooks and items needed to finish a piece of jewellery. These should tone with the beads unless you want to make a feature of them. Silver should be used for cool colour schemes and gold for warm colour schemes. Also available are coloured wires that can tone or contrast with the beads.

chapter two
COLOUR SCHEMES

This is a truly inspirational chapter! More than 150 items of beadwork including jewellery, vessels, tassels and objets d'art are used to illustrate the colour theory described in chapter one. Grouped into themed sections they show the beadworker how to be truly adventurous with colour. Each piece of beadwork has a corresponding graphic 'colour recipe' showing the proportions of the colours used to give an in-depth look at the dynamics of the colour scheme.

Eastern jade

BE INSPIRED BY JADE, WHICH IS A HIGHLY PRIZED STONE IN THE FAR EAST.

Jade, as a colour, is a saturated, slightly bluish green. The name comes from the jade stone, and although the stone varies widely in hue we mostly think of it as pale green. The turquoise and green colour schemes illustrated here have used this colour for inspiration.

TURQUOISE BROOCH
HEATHER KINGSLEY-HEATH
Shades of green, from pale to dark blue-green, have been used in this monochrome brooch. A triangular pattern is stitched around the brooch at the top, with a full fringe flowing from the bottom. The cabochon is held in place with rows of peyote stitch.

Turquoise 35%
Dark turquoise 15%
Yellow-green 10%
Dark blue 5%
Green turquoise 10%
Jade 5%
Mid jade 20%

GONE FISHING
ELISE MANN
The focal point of this elegant necklace is a beautiful carved jade pendant. It is strung on a spiral rope made from green, jade and pale gold seed beads. The jade seed beads match the jade pendant, while a darker green has been used to complete this monochromatic colour scheme.

Jade 40%
Pale gold 30%
Dark green 30%

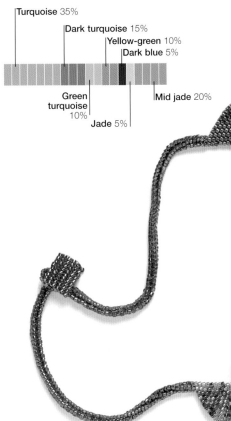

SUMMER NECKLACE
S. NEILSON

Spiral herringbone stitch has been used to make the sides of this necklace, which contains three beaded beads in the centre. The colours in this necklace are reminiscent of the sea and the sun – two tones of turquoise have been used together with gold as a highlight.

Pale turquoise 60%
Gold 20%
Pale blue-aqua 20%

PLAITED BRACELET
S. NEILSON

Three different shades of turquoise have been used in this bracelet. Each coloured seed bead – pale green-turquoise, blue-turquoise and very pale aqua – has been stitched into a long narrow band. The bands have then been plaited together. A button fastening has been added which complements the bracelet's colour scheme.

Blue-turquoise 35%
Very pale aqua 30%
Pale green-turquoise 35%

FANS AND BOWS
STEPHNEY HORNBLOW

Blue and green – the two colours either side of jade on the colour wheel – are often found together in the natural world and complement each other beautifully in this necklace. Stitched individual semicircles of beadwork in blue and green are strung together, the two sides brought together at the base with a carved blue cabochon.

Green 20%
Light blue 25%
Blue-green 20%
Blue 35%

Peacock feathers

PEACOCK FEATHERS HAVE A WONDERFUL ARRAY OF COLOURS TO TEMPT THE BEADER.

Peacocks are exquisite birds mainly because of the bright, iridescent colours and intricate patterns on their feathers, particularly the striking 'eye' pattern. Blue and purple, green, gold and bronze are all there to be used in a wide variety of ways. Apart from the colours, the iridescence of the feathers entices the beader to strive to capture the resemblance in his or her work.

Bright blue 10%
Green-blue 30%
Bronze 15%
Grey 5%
Black 5%
Dark bronze 5%
Green-grey 10%
Gold 20%

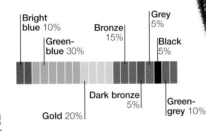

PEACOCK FEATHERS
SYLVIA FAIRHURST
This complementary colour scheme is very luxurious with darkened shades of bronze and blue. The lovely V-shaped fringe adds sparkle and matches the strap, with paler tones used to lighten the overall effect.

PEACOCK PURSE
ELISE MANN
The design of this diamond-shaped purse is symbolic and abstract. The 'eye' and feathers are representational, allowing the blue and green colouring and shape to dominate. The plain peyote strap suits the abstract design perfectly.

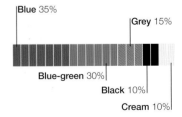

Blue 35%
Grey 15%
Blue-green 30%
Black 10%
Cream 10%

FEATHER EARRINGS
GILL HOOPER

These brick stitch earrings feature bright colours and a combination of matt and iris beads. This complementary colour scheme is a very bright version of the peacock's feathers. This is a lovely design that uses the colours and patterns in a miniature way.

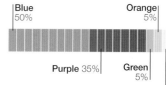

Blue 50%
Orange 5%
Purple 35%
Green 5%
Yellow 5%

THE EYE OF THE PEACOCK
SANDRA WALLACE

If you look closely at a feather, you will see that there are matt as well as iridescent areas. In this necklace, Aurora Borealis (AB) coated beads provide the iridescent shine, but there are also matt areas for contrast. This split loom necklace has a textural fringe, which balances the strung sections in the straps.

CRYSTAL RING
MELANIE DE MIGUEL

This analogous colour scheme is reminiscent of the peacock's colouring. Teal green and purple crystals sparkle and shine in this charming design. The corresponding seed beads used to stitch this ring tie in with the crystals beautifully.

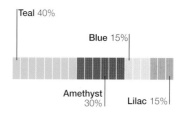

Teal 40%
Blue 15%
Amethyst 30%
Lilac 15%

Green-blue 50%
Lavender 5%
Mustard 10%
Blue-purple 5%
Dark green 15%
Dark purple 10%
Navy 5%

Bluebell woods

**ONE OF NATURE'S MOST STUNNING
DISPLAYS IS A CARPET OF BLUEBELLS.**

The purple-blue, bell-shaped flowers with their lush green
leaves canopied beneath the woodland trees are a beautiful
sight in the springtime. Most people love blue colour schemes
as they are particularly calming and create a sense of well-
being. The pieces on these two pages show a variety of colour
and design that is inspirational.

BLUE CATERPILLAR
CLAIRE CROUCHLEY
The dense textural fringe of this
bracelet is reminiscent of a furry
caterpillar. There are some wonderful
tints and shades of blue in this colour
scheme, and the variety of finishes
combined with the silver makes this
an eye-catching bracelet.

Navy 10%
Royal blue 15%
Silver 15%
Blue 15%
Mauve 10%
Pale blue 15%
Turquoise 20%

BEADED FUN
SUE STALLARD
An analogous colour scheme of blue
seed beads is used to create the spiral
rope. However, the focal point of this
necklace is the wonderful beaded
bead. The bead is embellished with a
variety of beads and crystals ranging
from turquoise through blue to lilac.
This gives the bead a textural finish
without being too elaborate.

Turquoise 55%
Blue 40%
Lilac 5%

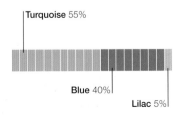

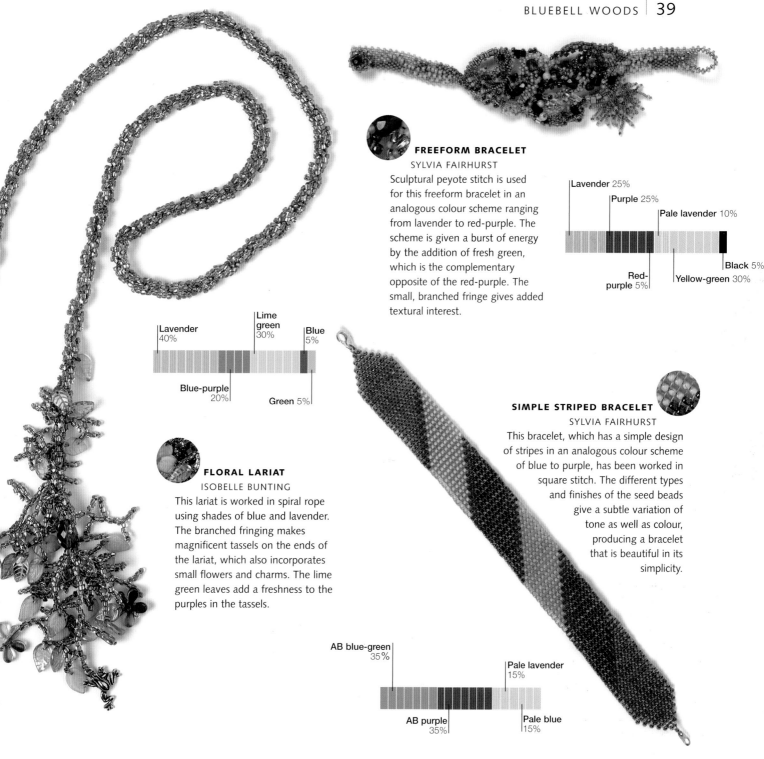

FREEFORM BRACELET

SYLVIA FAIRHURST

Sculptural peyote stitch is used for this freeform bracelet in an analogous colour scheme ranging from lavender to red-purple. The scheme is given a burst of energy by the addition of fresh green, which is the complementary opposite of the red-purple. The small, branched fringe gives added textural interest.

Lavender 25%
Purple 25%
Pale lavender 10%
Black 5%
Red-purple 5%
Yellow-green 30%

Lavender 40%
Lime green 30%
Blue 5%
Blue-purple 20%
Green 5%

FLORAL LARIAT

ISOBELLE BUNTING

This lariat is worked in spiral rope using shades of blue and lavender. The branched fringing makes magnificent tassels on the ends of the lariat, which also incorporates small flowers and charms. The lime green leaves add a freshness to the purples in the tassels.

SIMPLE STRIPED BRACELET

SYLVIA FAIRHURST

This bracelet, which has a simple design of stripes in an analogous colour scheme of blue to purple, has been worked in square stitch. The different types and finishes of the seed beads give a subtle variation of tone as well as colour, producing a bracelet that is beautiful in its simplicity.

AB blue-green 35%
Pale lavender 15%
AB purple 35%
Pale blue 15%

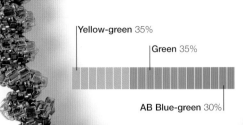

Forest glen

GREEN, THE COLOUR OF NATURE, MAKES US FEEL REFRESHED AND RENEWED.

Some greens, such as the fresh greens of springtime, invigorate us, whereas darker, richer greens are more elegant. Forest glen conjures up images of all shades of green, from the darker greens in the depth of the forest to the yellow-greens in the sunny glens.

Yellow-green 35%

Green 35%

AB Blue-green 30%

GREEN HERRINGBONE ROPE
BAR BLAKEY

Although there are many colours and finishes of bead in this herringbone rope, the different sections flow beautifully from one to the next. There is so much interest and variety yet no single section dominates. Larger beads are used to make the broader sections along the rope, with twisted Venetian-glass beads providing focal points.

Lime green 30%

Green 30%

Blue-green 5%

Very dark green 10%

Very pale green 10%

Moss green 5%

Leaf green 10%

TWISTING TORNADO
JENNY BOYLE

The colour scheme for this necklace is inspired by a dichroic pendant, which is used as a focal point. The colours of the spiral rope range from blue-green to yellow-green. The back of the necklace is plain, allowing for comfort around the neck, but the front uses a variation in size of bead to produce texture in the spiral.

Green-tinted white
25%

Blue-green
25%

Very dark green
15%

Dark green
25%

Very pale green
10%

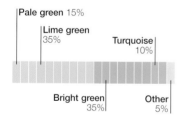

Pale green 15%

Lime green
35%

Turquoise
10%

Bright green
35%

Other
5%

GREEN PARTY POT

HEATHER KINGSLEY-HEATH

This adorable pot is made in brick stitch using a number of shades of bright green. The analogous colour scheme has greens ranging from lime green to turquoise in a series of stripes. There are a number of different sizes and finishes of bead, which provide texture to the pot.

WOODLAND GLADE

SANDRA WALLACE

Right-angle weaving has been used to make this simple bracelet. A matt green bead has been chosen for the foundation row, which is then embellished. Very dark green seed beads combine with all the colours of the forest to decorate the basic strand. The bracelet is fastened with a beaded bead.

Very dark green
30%

Yellow-green
20%

Green 40%

Pale green
10%

OCEAN BREEZE

HEATHER FENN-EDWARDS

The green hues used in this monochromatic colour scheme are muted, making this necklace very stylish. The design is well-balanced, with two spiral ropes on one side of an embellished pendant and a bold peyote spiral on the other side. Stone chips in the spiral rope create further interest.

Seascape tones

BORROW FROM NATURE AND USE THE COLOURS OF THE SEA.

Everyone loves a seascape, whether it's a powerful stormy sea or serenely calm blue waters. The pieces on these two pages show the sea in all its glory. Blue is a very wearable colour that suits everyone; it's just a matter of finding the right tone.

ABALONE SHELL
BERYL HARLAND

The analogous colour scheme for this necklace is taken from abalone shells. Nature has a wonderful way of using colour, and you can't go wrong following her example. The light and dark green tones dominate the necklace, while blue and mauve add interest and variety. The two-tone green herringbone tube allows the abalone shells with their seaweed fringing to take centre stage.

COOL BLUE GLASS
PAULINE HOLT

These handmade lampwork beads are a prime example of a cool colour scheme. It's not quite monochrome; the colours range from blue to turquoise with some tints and shades. The various sizes of the beads and their patterns add interest and texture, giving the appearance of a pebble beach.

Deep turquoise 30%

Turquoise 20%

Bright blue 25%

White 25%

BLUE SEAWEED
JAN NEWBERRY

This is an analogous colour scheme from blue to blue-green. The tonal values are similar along most of the necklace's length. The seaweed-like texture makes up for what the piece lacks in contrast. The advantage to the beader is the variety of finishes that are available in a narrow range of colours.

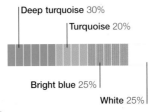

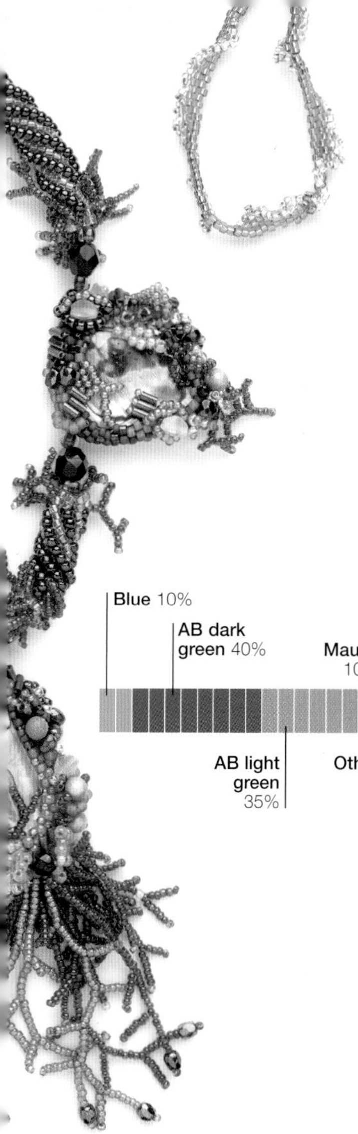

Silver blue 10%

Clear AB 10%

Shell 10%

Pale turquoise 20%

Dark turquoise 20%

Teal 20%

Other 10%

Blue 10%

AB dark green 40%

Mauve 10%

AB light green 35%

Other 5%

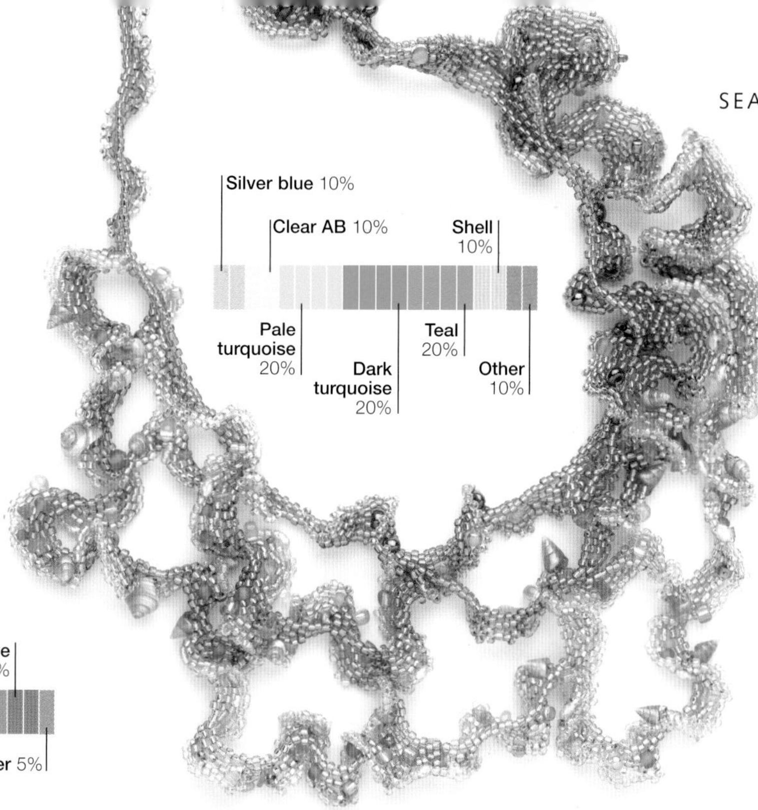

STORMY SEAS
CAROL BLACKBURN

This elegant necklace uses cool metallic silver to enhance the navy and greys in the peyote spiral, while the clear and frosted beads add extra contrast in texture and colour. The chunky spiral peyote in the centre is like a stormy sea with the surf rolling in. This is a neutral monochromatic colour scheme.

MONOCHROME RIPPLES
CHRISTINE BLOXHAM

This monochromatic colour scheme is visually appealing. The silver beads and scattering of shells give further interest to what is already a very good use of colour. The tones of turquoise range from clear to teal, reminiscent of a calm sea. The peyote-stitch ruffles add extra texture and look like waves breaking on a beach.

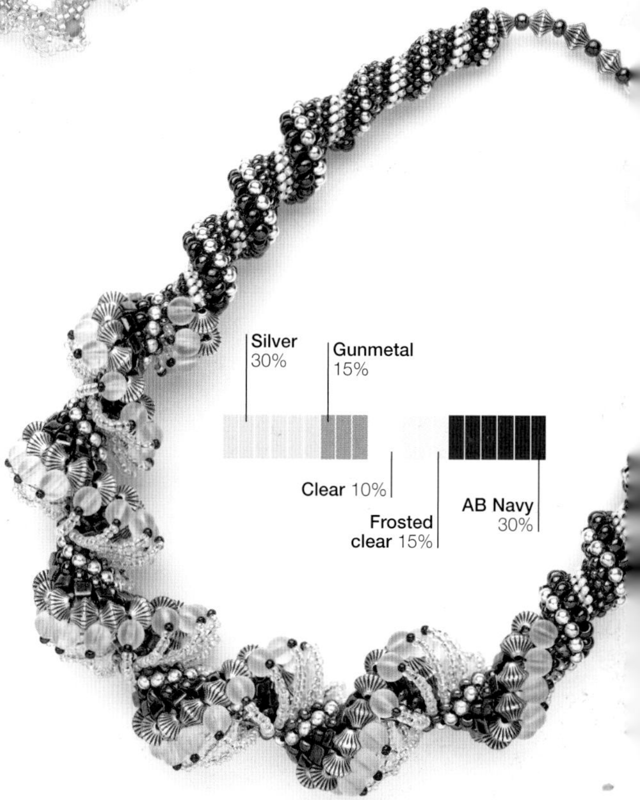

Silver 30%

Gunmetal 15%

Clear 10%

Frosted clear 15%

AB Navy 30%

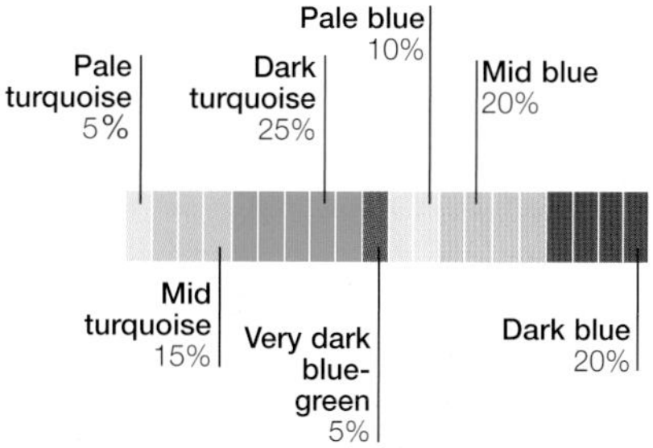

Pale blue 10%

Pale turquoise 5%

Dark turquoise 25%

Mid blue 20%

Mid turquoise 15%

Very dark blue-green 5%

Dark blue 20%

Volcano

WARM COLOURS HAVE A TENDENCY TO ADVANCE AND WILL DRAW ATTENTION TO THEMSELVES.

Warm colours are vivid, bold and exciting, and this is especially true of red and orange. These warm colours have a vibrancy of their own, and mixed with black they produce stunning colour schemes. Like volcanoes, which are very dramatic, the beadwork on these pages will definitely be noticed.

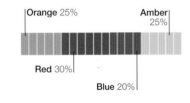

Orange 25%
Amber 25%
Red 30%
Blue 20%

LAVA
SANDRA WALLACE

The flowing lines of this dramatic necklace represent lava meandering its way down a volcano. The use of different finishes of seed beads in red, gunmetal and black gives depth to the design. The red and black lines of the flowing lava are carried through into the fringe, which comprises simple strands of seed beads.

ORANGE ZIGZAG
CLAIRE CROUCHLEY

The colours used in this decorative item are bursting with energy. The zigzag fringing adds extra texture to this fiery piece of beadwork, and it looks exactly like a volcano erupting. This is a complementary colour scheme, where the dark blue beads used as an accent colour create a stunning contrast to the orange.

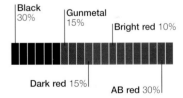

Black 30%
Gunmetal 15%
Bright red 10%
Dark red 15%
AB red 30%

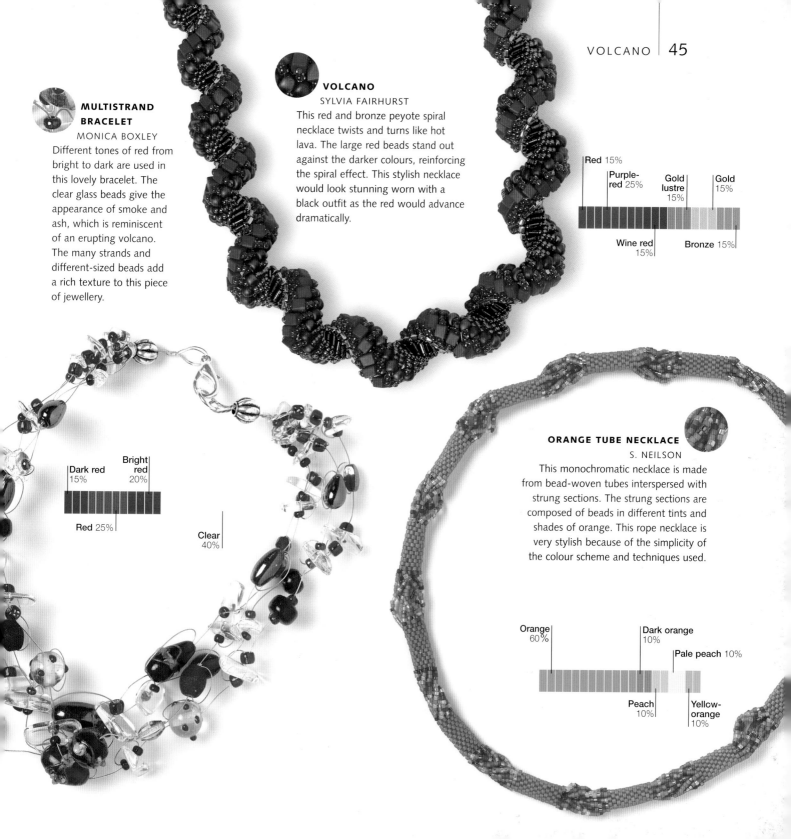

MULTISTRAND BRACELET
MONICA BOXLEY

Different tones of red from bright to dark are used in this lovely bracelet. The clear glass beads give the appearance of smoke and ash, which is reminiscent of an erupting volcano. The many strands and different-sized beads add a rich texture to this piece of jewellery.

VOLCANO
SYLVIA FAIRHURST

This red and bronze peyote spiral necklace twists and turns like hot lava. The large red beads stand out against the darker colours, reinforcing the spiral effect. This stylish necklace would look stunning worn with a black outfit as the red would advance dramatically.

Red 15%
Purple-red 25%
Gold lustre 15%
Gold 15%
Wine red 15%
Bronze 15%

Dark red 15%
Bright red 20%
Red 25%
Clear 40%

ORANGE TUBE NECKLACE
S. NEILSON

This monochromatic necklace is made from bead-woven tubes interspersed with strung sections. The strung sections are composed of beads in different tints and shades of orange. This rope necklace is very stylish because of the simplicity of the colour scheme and techniques used.

Orange 60%
Dark orange 10%
Pale peach 10%
Peach 10%
Yellow-orange 10%

New England fall

BE INSPIRED BY THE CHANGING COLOURS OF THE NEW ENGLAND LANDSCAPE IN FALL.

There is nothing quite like the spectacle of a New England fall. The glorious tones of the changing fall leaves paint the area in many variations of red, gold and amber. This colourful sight of blazing maples, golden beech trees and rich brown oaks is the perfect inspiration for a warm colour scheme for beaders.

INDIAN SPICE
HEATHER FENN-EDWARDS
This analogous colour scheme of golden-yellow and red echoes the brightness of fall foliage without being too vivid. The double spiral staircase is the perfect technique to show off these colours, which are echoed in the hanging pendant. The touch of gold in the pendant adds a degree of brightness to the focal point.

Gold 35%
Red 40%
Light green 10%
Silver 15%

CRYSTAL NECKLACE
S. NEILSON
This stylish necklace is strung with transparent faceted red glass and gleaming golden beads. The contrast of the red and gold is further emphasized by the addition of a few green beads. The silver findings tone down this necklace, making it very elegant rather than overdramatic.

Red 35%
Orange-red 10%
Purple 10%
Golden yellow 35%
Gold lustered cream 10%

DOORKNOBS

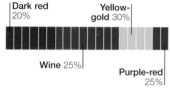

MELANIE DE MIGUEL

A wonderful way to display beadwork! These doorknobs, which are rich in colour, perfectly reflect the dark sumptuous colours of a traditional room. The eye is not distracted by pattern because the colours are blended freely in peyote stitch while the transparent beads add a radiance to the doorknob.

Dark red 20% Yellow-gold 30%
Wine 25% Purple-red 25%

ANGLESEY FALL

HEATHER FENN-EDWARDS

The glowing red and green complementary colours give a bright contrast to the more muted tones of the amber, red-orange and brown in the herringbone rope. The basic rope is then further embellished with leafy branched fringing, vines and glass leaves to give added texture and interest.

FALL FIRE

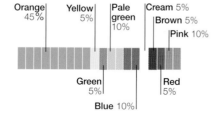

GILL HOOPER

The bright colours in this fun and fashionable bracelet reflect the glory of fall. Complementary blue and green beads have been added to the spiral rope to reflect the sky and evergreens, creating a contrast with the red and orange fall shades.

Orange 45% Yellow 5% Pale green 10% Cream 5% Brown 5% Pink 10%
Green 5% Red 5%
Blue 10%

Red-orange 30% Amber 10% Dark brown 10% Tan 10% Green 10%
Brown 15% White/clear 10%
Yellow-green 5%

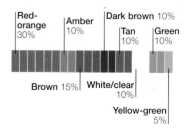

Sunset

SUNSETS ARE VIVID, AWE-INSPIRING AND MEMORABLE.

Sunsets range from vivid orange and yellow when the sun is low in the sky, to the wonderful pink and mauve seen when the sun has dropped below the horizon. Colour schemes range from analogous to complementary, and there is one here for everyone.

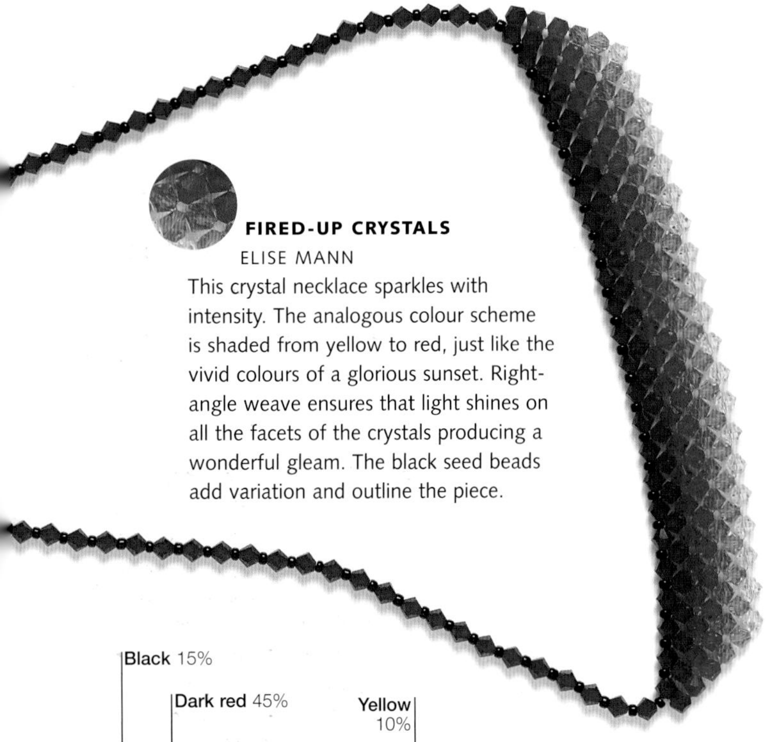

FIRED-UP CRYSTALS
ELISE MANN

This crystal necklace sparkles with intensity. The analogous colour scheme is shaded from yellow to red, just like the vivid colours of a glorious sunset. Right-angle weave ensures that light shines on all the facets of the crystals producing a wonderful gleam. The black seed beads add variation and outline the piece.

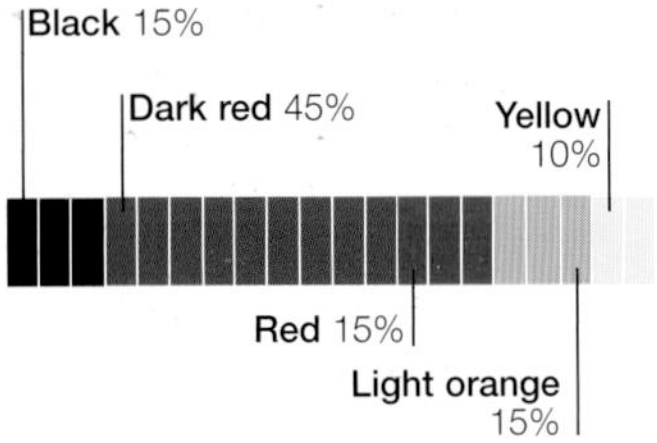

Black 15%
Dark red 45%
Yellow 10%
Red 15%
Light orange 15%

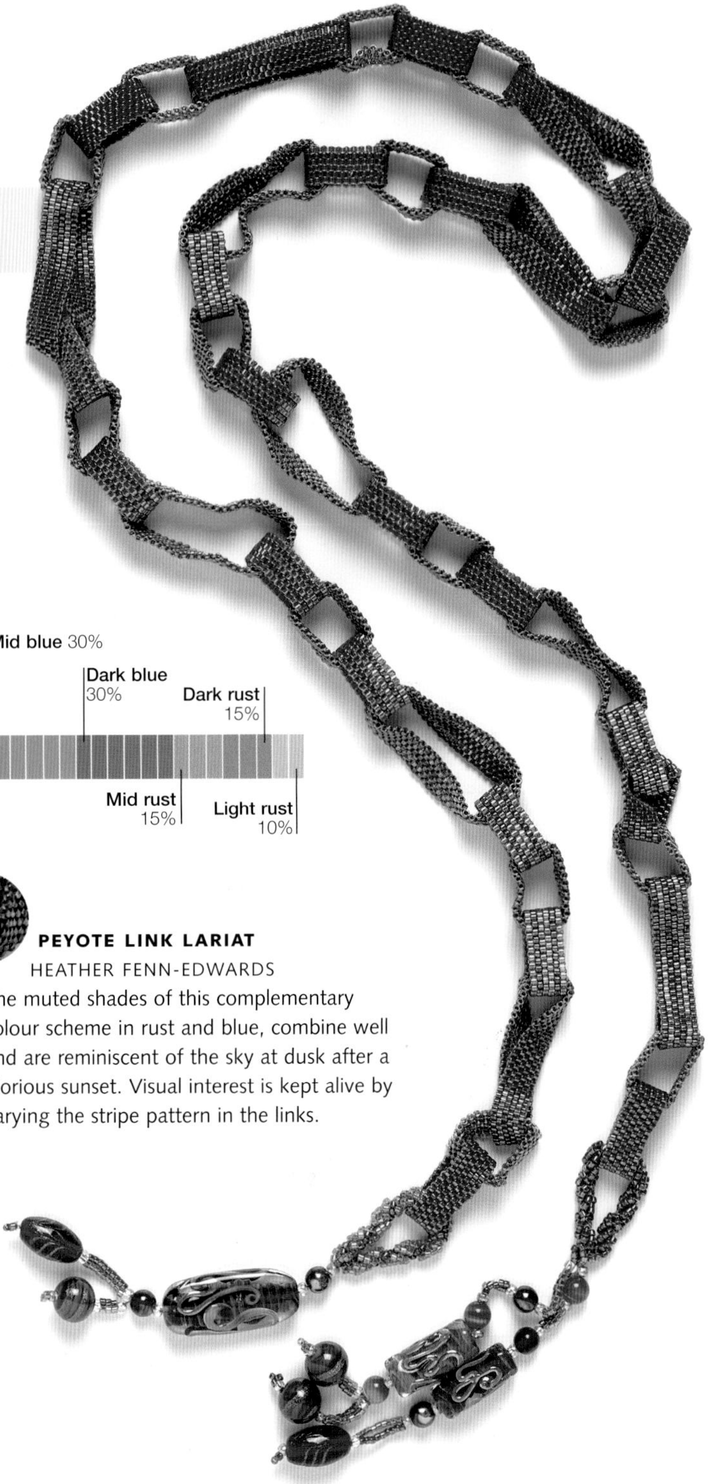

Mid blue 30%
Dark blue 30%
Dark rust 15%
Mid rust 15%
Light rust 10%

PEYOTE LINK LARIAT
HEATHER FENN-EDWARDS

The muted shades of this complementary colour scheme in rust and blue, combine well and are reminiscent of the sky at dusk after a glorious sunset. Visual interest is kept alive by varying the stripe pattern in the links.

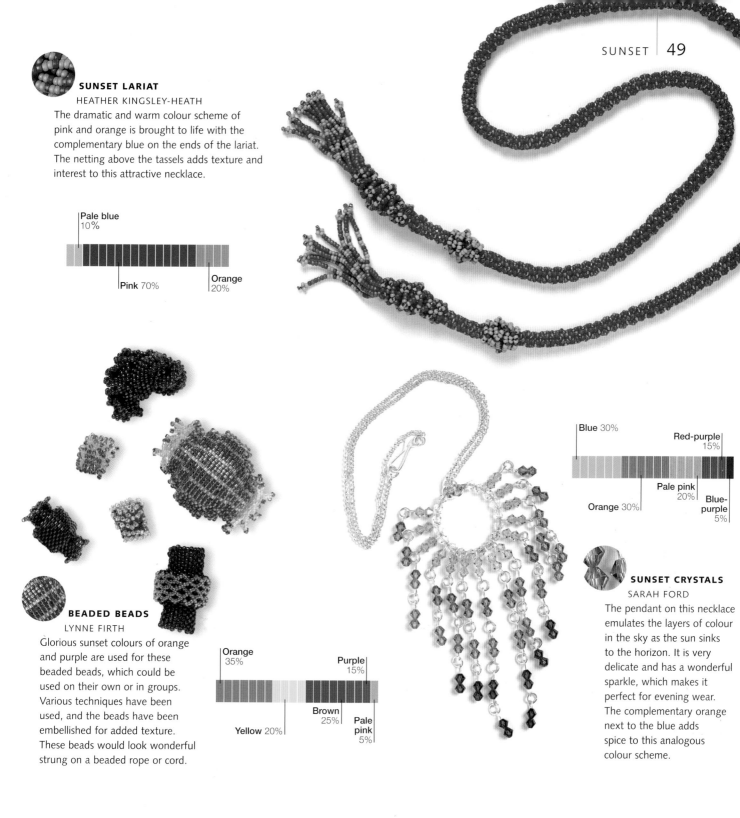

SUNSET LARIAT
HEATHER KINGSLEY-HEATH

The dramatic and warm colour scheme of pink and orange is brought to life with the complementary blue on the ends of the lariat. The netting above the tassels adds texture and interest to this attractive necklace.

Pale blue 10%

Pink 70%

Orange 20%

BEADED BEADS
LYNNE FIRTH

Glorious sunset colours of orange and purple are used for these beaded beads, which could be used on their own or in groups. Various techniques have been used, and the beads have been embellished for added texture. These beads would look wonderful strung on a beaded rope or cord.

Orange 35%

Yellow 20%

Brown 25%

Pale pink 5%

Purple 15%

Blue 30%

Orange 30%

Pale pink 20%

Blue-purple 5%

Red-purple 15%

SUNSET CRYSTALS
SARAH FORD

The pendant on this necklace emulates the layers of colour in the sky as the sun sinks to the horizon. It is very delicate and has a wonderful sparkle, which makes it perfect for evening wear. The complementary orange next to the blue adds spice to this analogous colour scheme.

Autumn leaves

AUTUMN IS THE SEASON OF GLOWING COLOURS AND RUSTLING LEAVES.

There is so much inspiration in the autumn, from the warm gold of harvest fields to the rich colours of the leaves and berries. Use these colour schemes with gold for elegance or tone them down using matt beads for everyday wear. However they are used, you can guarantee that you will have a splendid piece of jewellery.

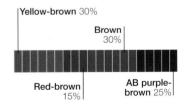

TOFFEE TEA LIGHT
JENNY WILSON
This tea light would make a lovely centrepiece for a dining table, with the rich brown beadwork surrounding the candle's flame. The toffee colours glow with the shiny glass beads. This analogous colour scheme in a freeform technique reveals the textures of autumn as well as the colours.

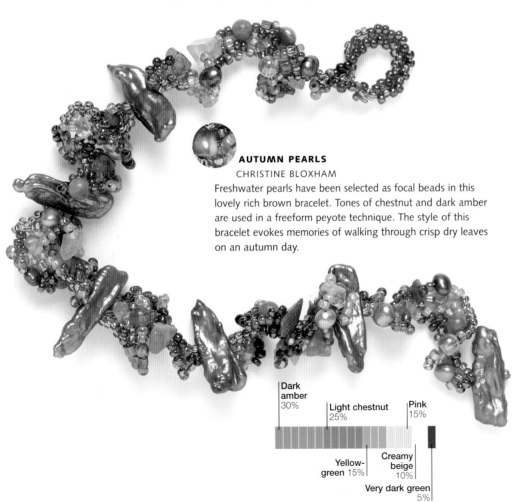

AUTUMN PEARLS
CHRISTINE BLOXHAM
Freshwater pearls have been selected as focal beads in this lovely rich brown bracelet. Tones of chestnut and dark amber are used in a freeform peyote technique. The style of this bracelet evokes memories of walking through crisp dry leaves on an autumn day.

Yellow-brown 30%

Brown 30%

Red-brown 15%

AB purple-brown 25%

Dark amber 30%

Light chestnut 25%

Pink 15%

Yellow-green 15%

Creamy beige 10%

Very dark green 5%

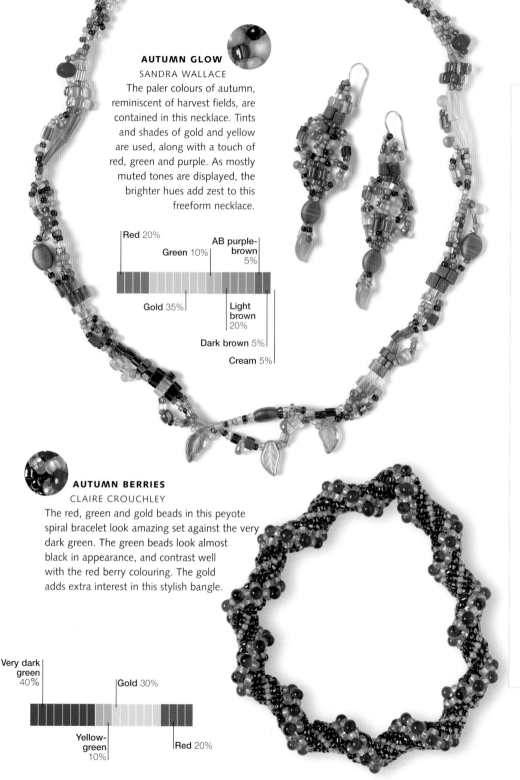

AUTUMN GLOW
SANDRA WALLACE

The paler colours of autumn, reminiscent of harvest fields, are contained in this necklace. Tints and shades of gold and yellow are used, along with a touch of red, green and purple. As mostly muted tones are displayed, the brighter hues add zest to this freeform necklace.

Red 20%
Green 10%
AB purple-brown 5%
Gold 35%
Light brown 20%
Dark brown 5%
Cream 5%

Brown 20%
Copper 15%
Red 5%
Olive green 10%
Rust 15%
Bronze 15%
Amber 15%
Very dark green 5%

HEDGEROW HARVEST
SANDRA WALLACE

The berries and rich brown beechnuts in autumn hedgerows inspired this brick stitch vessel. Using an analogous colour scheme in red, amber and shades of brown, with a few splashes of green for interest, this vessel uses a mixture of sizes of beads for texture.

AUTUMN BERRIES
CLAIRE CROUCHLEY

The red, green and gold beads in this peyote spiral bracelet look amazing set against the very dark green. The green beads look almost black in appearance, and contrast well with the red berry colouring. The gold adds extra interest in this stylish bangle.

Very dark green 40%
Gold 30%
Yellow-green 10%
Red 20%

Grand Canyon

THE COLOURS OF THE GRAND CANYON ARE AMAZING AND VARIED.

The colours in the Grand Canyon change according to the time of day and the quality of the light. The rocks can be any colour from peach to russet or pink to mauve. The wide selection of colours and textures found there can provide great inspiration for the beader.

GRAND CANYON
ANITA SEEBERG

The pink tones of the Grand Canyon are the inspiration for this necklace and bracelet set. Rhodonite, rose quartz, mookite and leopardskin jasper are combined with freshwater pearls and silver. A toning pink lampwork bead has been used as a focal point for the necklace, and a matching suede thong completes the piece.

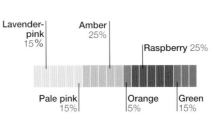

Lavender-pink 15% | Amber 25% | Raspberry 25%
Pale pink 15% | Orange 5% | Green 15%

CANYON FACETS
JANE SADGROVE

An assortment of shapes of small beads have been strung on burgundy coloured wire, which has then been knitted into a cuff. Analogous colours in shades of pink, orange and amber have been used together with a contrasting green.

Palest pink 20%
Pale pink 20%
Jasper orange 5%
Rhodonite 45%
Silver 10%

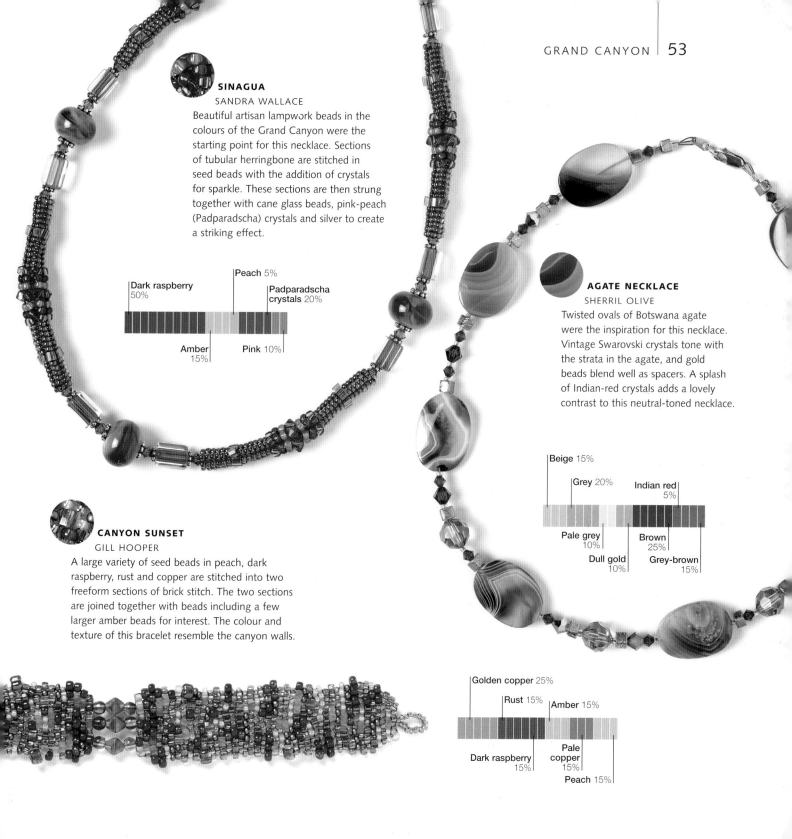

SINAGUA
SANDRA WALLACE

Beautiful artisan lampwork beads in the colours of the Grand Canyon were the starting point for this necklace. Sections of tubular herringbone are stitched in seed beads with the addition of crystals for sparkle. These sections are then strung together with cane glass beads, pink-peach (Padparadscha) crystals and silver to create a striking effect.

Dark raspberry 50%
Peach 5%
Padparadscha crystals 20%
Amber 15%
Pink 10%

AGATE NECKLACE
SHERRIL OLIVE

Twisted ovals of Botswana agate were the inspiration for this necklace. Vintage Swarovski crystals tone with the strata in the agate, and gold beads blend well as spacers. A splash of Indian-red crystals adds a lovely contrast to this neutral-toned necklace.

Beige 15%
Grey 20%
Indian red 5%
Pale grey 10%
Dull gold 10%
Brown 25%
Grey-brown 15%

CANYON SUNSET
GILL HOOPER

A large variety of seed beads in peach, dark raspberry, rust and copper are stitched into two freeform sections of brick stitch. The two sections are joined together with beads including a few larger amber beads for interest. The colour and texture of this bracelet resemble the canyon walls.

Golden copper 25%
Rust 15%
Amber 15%
Dark raspberry 15%
Pale copper 15%
Peach 15%

Stormy seas

STORMY SEAS ARE POWERFUL, MAJESTIC AND AWE-INSPIRING.

The colours of the sea are so varied, depending on the time of day and whether it is wet and windy, blustrey or blowing a gale. The shades are always muted in a stormy sea, and colours can range from grey and mauve to green and blue with off-white surf. Silver is the best metal to tone with a grey colour scheme.

Black 10%
Dark grey 15%
Blue 10%
Mid grey 15%
Pale grey 20%
Silver 10%
Blue-grey 20%

SPIRAL ROPE NECKLACE
HEATHER KINGSLEY-HEATH
This necklace has a monochromatic colour scheme in three shades of grey. Dark grey is used for the spiral rope, which is then embellished with discs in two tones of paler grey. The highlight of the necklace is the peyote discs, which are attached at random intervals along the rope.

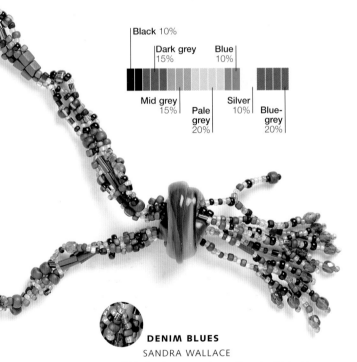

DENIM BLUES
SANDRA WALLACE
This freeform peyote necklace is stitched in a variety of beads for texture. Colours range from monochromatic pale grey to black, with accents of blue. The focal point is a handmade glass bead in shades of grey. This cool neutral colour scheme is well-suited to the moodiness of a stormy sea.

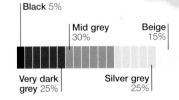

PEBBLE NECKLACE AND BROOCH
HEATHER KINGSLEY-HEATH
A pebble is used as the centrepiece for this necklace, instantly evoking images of the sea. The dark grey pebble is surrounded by peyote stitch in black and silver grey. The spiral rope harmonizes with the pebble in tone and simplicity of design.

Black 5%
Mid grey 30%
Beige 15%
Very dark grey 25%
Silver grey 25%

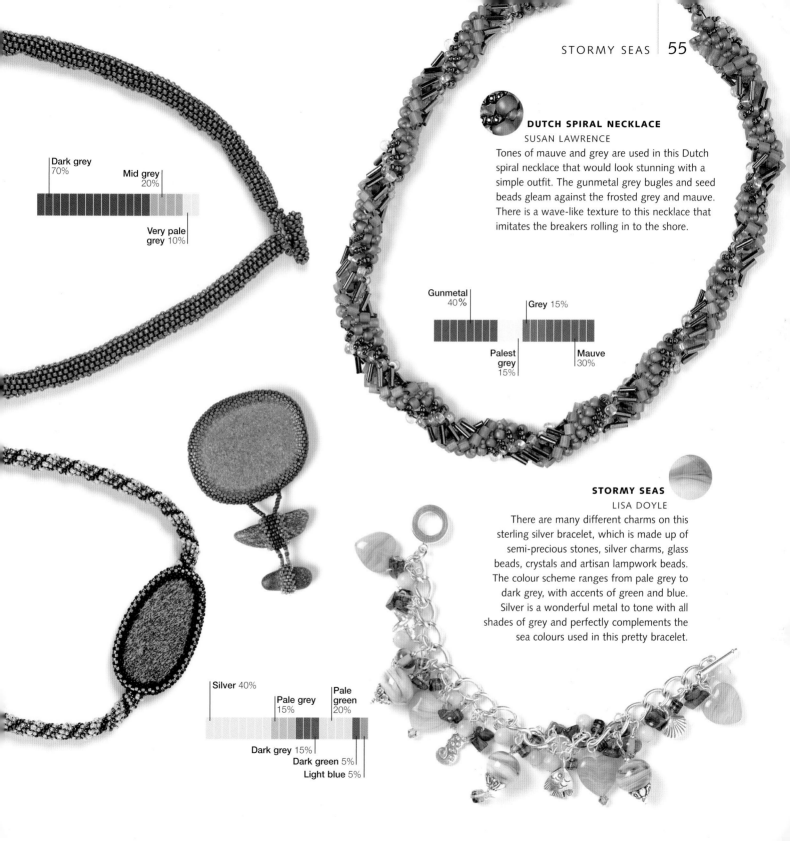

Dark grey
70%

Mid grey
20%

Very pale
grey 10%

DUTCH SPIRAL NECKLACE
SUSAN LAWRENCE

Tones of mauve and grey are used in this Dutch
spiral necklace that would look stunning with a
simple outfit. The gunmetal grey bugles and seed
beads gleam against the frosted grey and mauve.
There is a wave-like texture to this necklace that
imitates the breakers rolling in to the shore.

Gunmetal
40%

Grey 15%

Palest
grey
15%

Mauve
30%

STORMY SEAS
LISA DOYLE

There are many different charms on this
sterling silver bracelet, which is made up of
semi-precious stones, silver charms, glass
beads, crystals and artisan lampwork beads.
The colour scheme ranges from pale grey to
dark grey, with accents of green and blue.
Silver is a wonderful metal to tone with all
shades of grey and perfectly complements the
sea colours used in this pretty bracelet.

Silver 40%

Pale grey
15%

Pale
green
20%

Dark grey 15%

Dark green 5%

Light blue 5%

Dry stone wall

THE HUES USED HERE RANGE FROM WARM TO COOL, SO THERE IS SOMETHING FOR EVERYONE.

The English landscape has many dry stone walls separating fields and meadows. These walls vary in colour according to the part of the country they are located in and the local stones. This theme contains neutral beige, encompassing all shades from yellow-beige to grey-beige, and pale to dark.

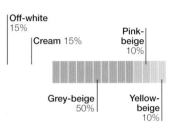

Off-white 15%
Cream 15%
Pink-beige 10%
Grey-beige 50%
Yellow-beige 10%

PEYOTE RUFFLE NECKLACE

HEATHER KINGSLEY-HEATH

This simple but stunning peyote necklace, which takes its colour scheme from the long shell beads, uses off-white to grey-beige seed beads. The beads are stitched in such a way that the peyote band ruffles slightly between them. The neutral colour scheme will go well with warm or cool colours.

MACRAMÉ NECKLACE

JANE OLSEN-PHILLIPS

This macramé necklace is bursting with wonderful texture. Two shades of beige cord have been used, together with a few beige beads and an abundance of bright blue and green beads to add interest. Blue is the complementary colour for the darker beige, so it works very well here. The two sides come together and meet with a wonderful focal bead.

Pale beige 40%
Light caramel 30%
Blue 5%
Pale green 5%
Yellow 10%
Green 5%
Purple 5%

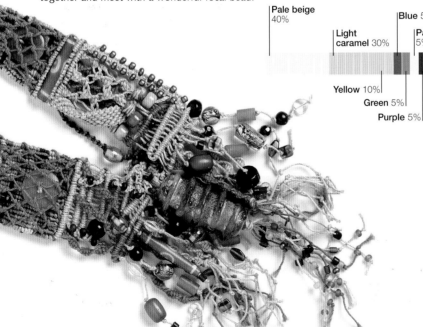

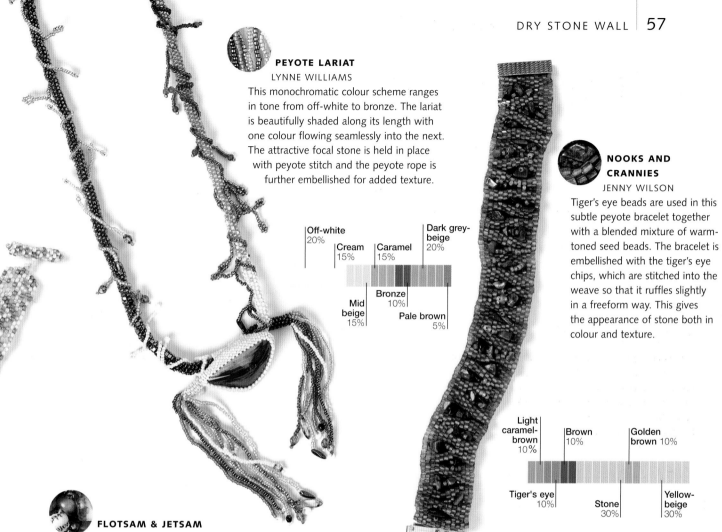

PEYOTE LARIAT
LYNNE WILLIAMS

This monochromatic colour scheme ranges
in tone from off-white to bronze. The lariat
is beautifully shaded along its length with
one colour flowing seamlessly into the next.
The attractive focal stone is held in place
with peyote stitch and the peyote rope is
further embellished for added texture.

Off-white
20%
Cream
15%
Caramel
15%
Dark grey-
beige
20%
Mid
beige
15%
Bronze
10%
Pale brown
5%

NOOKS AND CRANNIES
JENNY WILSON

Tiger's eye beads are used in this
subtle peyote bracelet together
with a blended mixture of warm-
toned seed beads. The bracelet is
embellished with the tiger's eye
chips, which are stitched into the
weave so that it ruffles slightly
in a freeform way. This gives
the appearance of stone both in
colour and texture.

Light
caramel-
brown
10%
Brown
10%
Golden
brown 10%
Tiger's eye
10%
Stone
30%
Yellow-
beige
30%

FLOTSAM & JETSAM
JENNY WILSON

The base of this square stitch bracelet is made from
grey-beige seed beads. The band is then embellished
with a variety of semi-precious stone chips in grey and
white. There is further embellishment with seed and bugle
beads around the stones, and a few branched fringes in
bright green complete the effect.

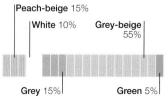

Peach-beige 15%
White 10%
Grey-beige
55%
Grey 15%
Green 5%

Crème de la crème

THESE ITEMS OF JEWELLERY ARE THE PINNACLE OF STYLE.

Cream and off-white are the most versatile of neutrals and can be paired with any other colour. Warm creams are best paired with warm colours and earth tones, while off-white or ivory tones are much easier to use than stark brilliant white. Everyone should have at least one item of jewellery in this adaptable neutral colouring.

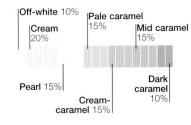

CRÈME CARAMEL
SUE MAGUIRE

This wonderful lariat has tones ranging from off-white to caramel in almost equal proportions. There is an abundance of texture in the leafy, feather-like fringing, which is fuller towards the ends. These cream and caramel colours make this a very versatile and stylish necklace.

White 5%

Off-white 90%

Grey-beige 5%

BUTTON NECKLACE
HEATHER KINGSLEY-HEATH

The focus of this necklace is the pearl button, which is used to fasten the necklace at the front. Off-white lustred beads have been used for the peyote spiral rope. The ends of the rope have been embellished for texture and appeal.

Off-white 10%

Cream 20%

Pale caramel 15%

Mid caramel 15%

Pearl 15%

Cream-caramel 15%

Dark caramel 10%

SHELL BRACELET
KATI TORDA

Off-white is a lovely neutral that will go well with any colour. It is softer than brilliant white and more versatile; paired with black it is dramatic but not harsh. This multi-stranded shell bracelet is strung on a knotted cord, which incorporates black beads. The ends are finished with warm-toned brass beads.

Brass 10%

Black 20%

Pinky-beige 10%

Off-white 60%

CREAM RIBBON
PAT ROSS

Cream and gold are the perfect combination for a stylish necklace. This lariat is a luscious ribbon of cream lustred beads edged with a gold picot. A subtle fringe finishes the ends perfectly. Pure understated elegance!

Cream 75%

Gold 25%

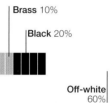

BROOCH
HEATHER KINGSLEY-HEATH

A delightful moon face has been chosen for the centre of this brooch. The matt finish of the face is repeated in the beads that surround it. Lustred and shiny beads have been added for variation, together with flat beads A pretty picot edging completes the brooch.

Off-white 25%

Pale cream 30%

Pale gold 20%

Beige 25%

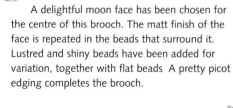

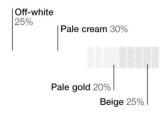

Floral fantasy

IT IS DELIGHTFUL TO SEE THE FIRST SPRING
FLOWERS AFTER A BLEAK WINTER.

These flowers are guaranteed to bring a smile to
your face. Here you will find vivid, bold flowers
commanding attention, as well as soft and delicate
creations that are more subtle. Whatever your taste,
there is a floral scheme here for you.

SERPENTINE BOUQUET
SUE STALLARD
Aurora Borealis (AB) finished blue-green beads have been
used to make the herringbone rope, which serves as a
backdrop for these vivid flowers. Bright red, magenta and
blue have been combined in these flowers, which
have the appearance of carnations. The link
between all the flowers is a turquoise-blue
edging to the petals.

DAISY BARRETTE
DANI CROMPTON
A hair decoration is a lovely
way to wear beadwork. This
is a very simple colour scheme
of pale and dark raspberry-
pinks; the beauty lies in the
composition of the design.
It is an open design, but the
overlapping of the petals and
the use of colour in the loops
give the appearance of a
more complex design.

Raspberry
40%

Pale pink
30%

Mid pink
30%

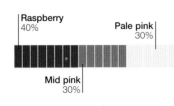

AB blue-green
55%

Dusky pink
5%

Mid blue
5%

Red 10%

Blue 10%

Magenta
10%

Turquoise 5%

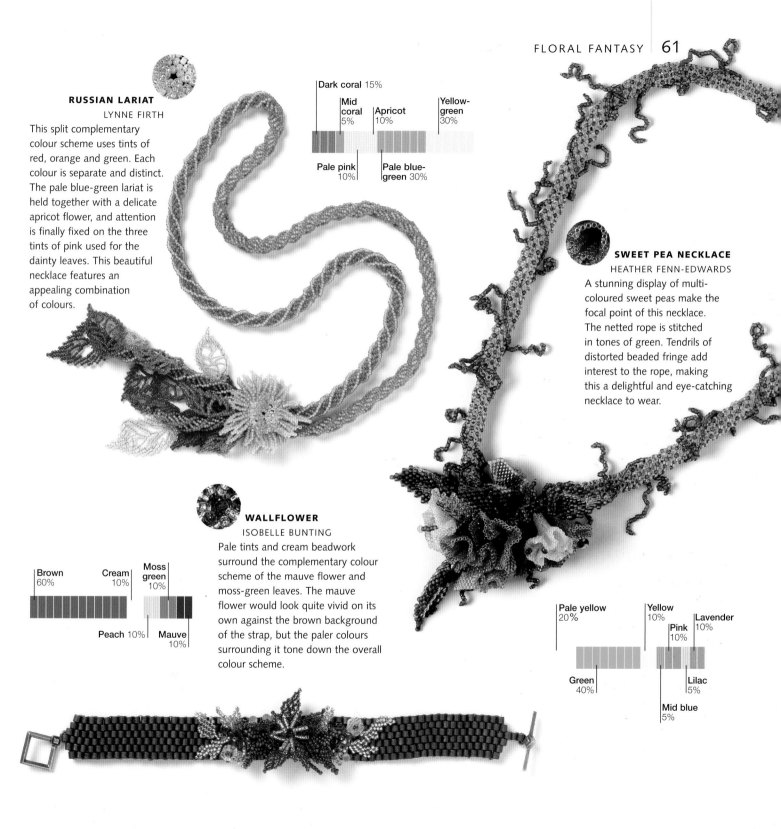

RUSSIAN LARIAT
LYNNE FIRTH

This split complementary colour scheme uses tints of red, orange and green. Each colour is separate and distinct. The pale blue-green lariat is held together with a delicate apricot flower, and attention is finally fixed on the three tints of pink used for the dainty leaves. This beautiful necklace features an appealing combination of colours.

Dark coral 15%
Mid coral 5%
Apricot 10%
Yellow-green 30%
Pale pink 10%
Pale blue-green 30%

SWEET PEA NECKLACE
HEATHER FENN-EDWARDS

A stunning display of multi-coloured sweet peas make the focal point of this necklace. The netted rope is stitched in tones of green. Tendrils of distorted beaded fringe add interest to the rope, making this a delightful and eye-catching necklace to wear.

WALLFLOWER
ISOBELLE BUNTING

Pale tints and cream beadwork surround the complementary colour scheme of the mauve flower and moss-green leaves. The mauve flower would look quite vivid on its own against the brown background of the strap, but the paler colours surrounding it tone down the overall colour scheme.

Brown 60%
Cream 10%
Moss green 10%
Peach 10%
Mauve 10%

Pale yellow 20%
Yellow 10%
Pink 10%
Lavender 10%
Green 40%
Lilac 5%
Mid blue 5%

Candy store

SOMETHING TO APPEAL TO EVERY TASTE AND MAKE YOUR MOUTH WATER.

To satisfy all the bead addicts, this is a selection of jewellery and beads in a variety of colours, sizes, shapes and textures. Here we have everything from pastel to bright, textured to smooth, large to small.

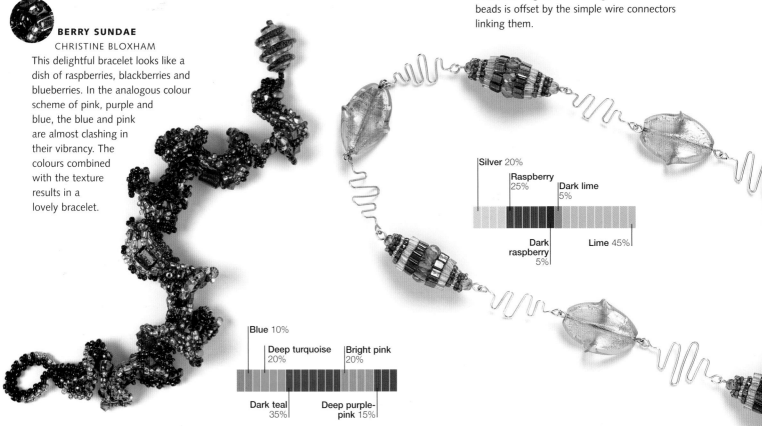

RASPBERRY AND LIME
SANDRA WALLACE

Red-purple and yellow-green is a delicious combination of complementary colours. The beaded beads perfectly echo the lime green in the Venetian-glass beads. The beaded beads are bright, but the brightness of the beads is offset by the simple wire connectors linking them.

BERRY SUNDAE
CHRISTINE BLOXHAM

This delightful bracelet looks like a dish of raspberries, blackberries and blueberries. In the analogous colour scheme of pink, purple and blue, the blue and pink are almost clashing in their vibrancy. The colours combined with the texture results in a lovely bracelet.

Silver 20%

Raspberry 25%   Dark lime 5%

Dark raspberry 5%   Lime 45%

Blue 10%

Deep turquoise 20%   Bright pink 20%

Dark teal 35%   Deep purple-pink 15%

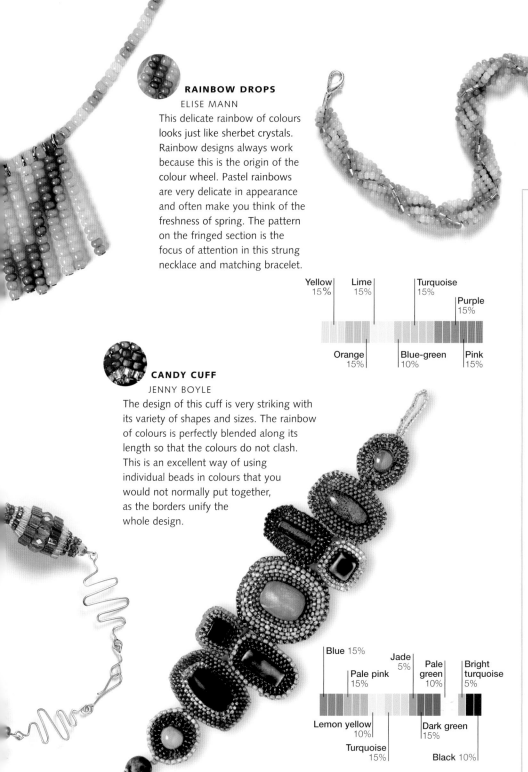

RAINBOW DROPS
ELISE MANN

This delicate rainbow of colours looks just like sherbet crystals. Rainbow designs always work because this is the origin of the colour wheel. Pastel rainbows are very delicate in appearance and often make you think of the freshness of spring. The pattern on the fringed section is the focus of attention in this strung necklace and matching bracelet.

Yellow 15%	Lime 15%		Turquoise 15%		Purple 15%
Orange 15%		Blue-green 10%		Pink 15%	

CANDY CUFF
JENNY BOYLE

The design of this cuff is very striking with its variety of shapes and sizes. The rainbow of colours is perfectly blended along its length so that the colours do not clash. This is an excellent way of using individual beads in colours that you would not normally put together, as the borders unify the whole design.

Blue 15%		Jade 5%		Pale green 10%		Bright turquoise 5%
Pale pink 15%						
Lemon yellow 10%				Dark green 15%		
Turquoise 15%				Black 10%		

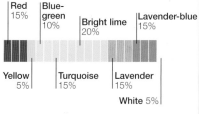

Red 15%	Blue-green 10%		Bright lime 20%		Lavender-blue 15%
Yellow 5%	Turquoise 15%		Lavender 15%		White 5%

BRIGHT BEADS
PAULINE HOLT

These handmade glass beads are wonderfully colourful and bright – analogous colours of blue and purple are mixed with complementary red and green. The colour schemes of some of the beads are almost split complementary, while others are almost tertiary. These beads show that rules are sometimes meant to be broken!

Summer garden

As well as ideas for colour schemes, beaders can find textural interest in the garden.

Traditional flower borders are a delightful riot of colour. Nature has a wonderful way of harmonizing by setting a rainbow of colours against a backdrop of green, enabling colours that would normally clash to reside together in harmony. Here we see a wonderful array of jewellery inspired by a summer garden.

FLORAL PURSE
CLAIRE CROUCHLEY
The highlight of this purse is the bright yellow flower centre, which complements the purple petals. The beautiful shading in the petals, which are set against the green background, continues into the fringe, producing a cohesive design. The simplicity of the beaded necklace strap balances the abundance of fringe perfectly.

GARDEN CATERPILLAR
CLAIRE CROUCHLEY
This textural bracelet resembles a floral border containing little blue and yellow flowers. Several shades of blue and green are used to give depth to the colour scheme. Pretty little flower beads add a difference in texture, and the subtle red and yellow tones add contrast to the scheme.

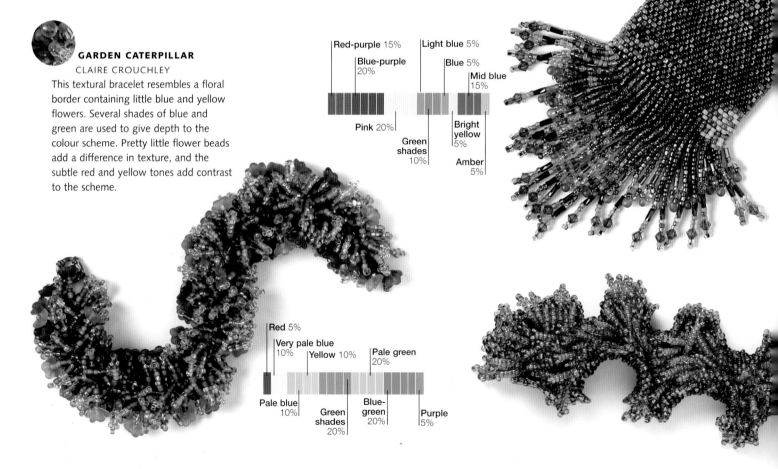

Red-purple 15%

Blue-purple 20%

Light blue 5%

Blue 5%

Mid blue 15%

Pink 20%

Green shades 10%

Bright yellow 5%

Amber 5%

Red 5%

Very pale blue 10%

Yellow 10%

Pale green 20%

Pale blue 10%

Green shades 20%

Blue-green 20%

Purple 5%

SUMMERTIME
SANDRA WALLACE

This delicate colour scheme mostly uses pastel hues of different shades of blue and pink with a little green for contrast. The necklace is stitched with a variety of beads, which add texture to the freeform peyote. This is a summer necklace, recalling images of an English garden.

Blue hues 20%
Turquoise 15%
Lilac 25%
Pink 25%
Raspberry 5%
Yellow-green 5%
Pastel blue-green 5%

Lavender blue 30%
Turquoise 20%
Mauve 25%
Mid green 15%
Red-purple 10%

DAISY CHAIN
S. NEILSON

This casual and fun bracelet would look good with denim. The carpet of green is overlaid with daisies in a multitude of colours. These colours also form a decorative edging on each side, but the whole effect works well because of the plain background.

CUFF
HEATHER KINGSLEY-HEATH

The deep texture in this piece has been created by the wavy peyote stitch and the fringing. The cuff uses a broad analogous colour scheme of purple through blue to green. The blue and purple are reminiscent of garden flowers, with a trace of green edging on the fringe to resemble leaves.

Mid green 55%
Bright yellow 5%
Soft-hued blue 5%
Dark blue 5%
Pink 5%
Red 5%
Raspberry 5%
White 5%
Orange 5%
Lavender 5%

Down to earth

THE ATTRACTIVE BEADWORK HERE SHOWS THAT EARTH TONES CAN LOOK STUNNING.

Tones of umber, ochre and sienna are the colours that we associate most with 'mother earth'. These muted hues often have a mixture of the primary colours and can be either warm or cool. The cool hues have a proportion of blue in their composition, and olive green and grey-blue often blend well with this palette.

PEARL BRACELET
HEATHER FENN-EDWARDS

Freshwater pearls are contrasted with matt square beads in this stylish ladder stitch bracelet. The bracelet is then outlined with drop beads and pink Ceylon beads. The colour of the seed beads brightens up the dark colours in the bracelet, making it really quite elegant.

JURASSIC GEMS
JENNY BOYLE

Using fossils as a focal feature is an ideal starting point for an earth tone necklace. The colours in the fossils are reproduced in the sculptural beadwork surrounding them. Similar tones are then echoed in the various spirals of the necklace. Although there's a great variety here, the balance is perfect.

Pale grey 15%
Light brown 15%
Dark grey-brown 10%
Rust 10%
Amber/gold 45%
Pink-brown 5%

Brass 15%
Cream 10%
Terracotta 10%
Grey-brown 10%
Off-white 15%
Dark terracotta 15%
Beige 25%

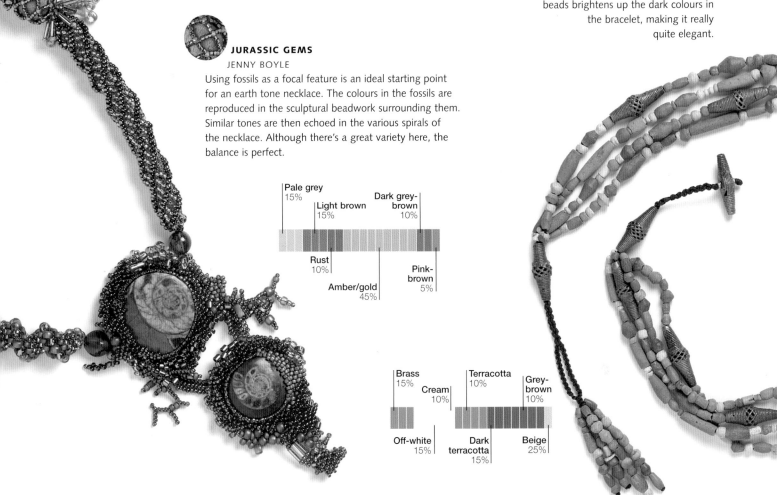

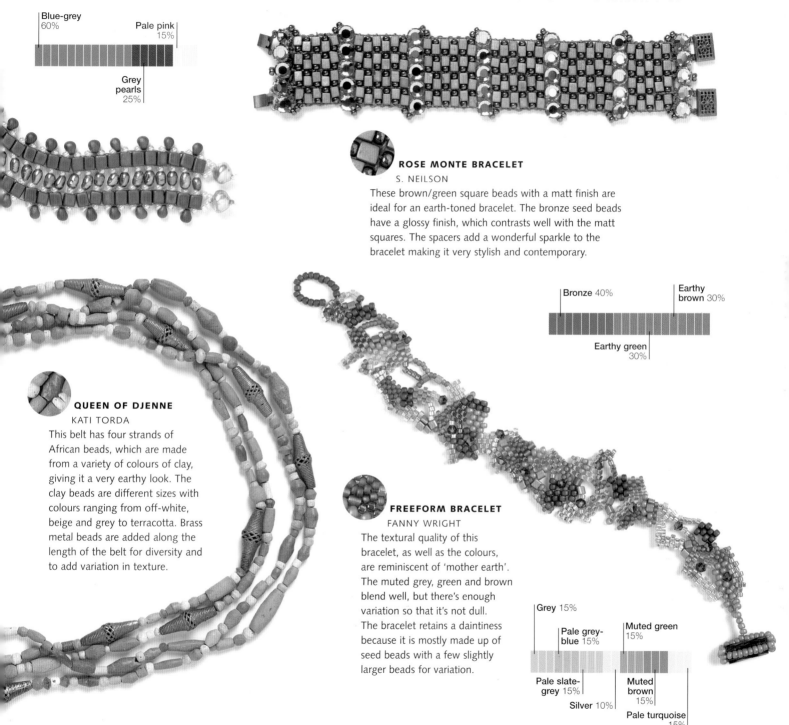

Blue-grey 60%   Pale pink 15%
Grey pearls 25%

ROSE MONTE BRACELET
S. NEILSON

These brown/green square beads with a matt finish are ideal for an earth-toned bracelet. The bronze seed beads have a glossy finish, which contrasts well with the matt squares. The spacers add a wonderful sparkle to the bracelet making it very stylish and contemporary.

Bronze 40%   Earthy brown 30%
Earthy green 30%

QUEEN OF DJENNE
KATI TORDA

This belt has four strands of African beads, which are made from a variety of colours of clay, giving it a very earthy look. The clay beads are different sizes with colours ranging from off-white, beige and grey to terracotta. Brass metal beads are added along the length of the belt for diversity and to add variation in texture.

FREEFORM BRACELET
FANNY WRIGHT

The textural quality of this bracelet, as well as the colours, are reminiscent of 'mother earth'. The muted grey, green and brown blend well, but there's enough variation so that it's not dull. The bracelet retains a daintiness because it is mostly made up of seed beads with a few slightly larger beads for variation.

Grey 15%
Pale grey-blue 15%
Muted green 15%
Pale slate-grey 15%
Silver 10%
Muted brown 15%
Pale turquoise 15%

Dawn mist

EARLY DAWN HAS AN AMBIENCE THAT IS UNIQUE AND MOOD-ENHANCING.

Dawn can vary from clear days with pink and lavender skies to grey and misty days when it is not easy to see any colour at all. The sun is often weak and watery so colours are faint too. Greyed lavender and pink are typical colours for early dawn, and in this theme you will find pale tints as well as hues that are low in saturation.

MULTI-STRAND NECKLACE
CHRISTINE BLOXHAM

Pale blue-grey is the background colour for this attractive necklace. The twisted sections separate at the front into several strands that are intertwined. Larger beads and pearls are added along the length and in the strands.

PINK DAWN
SANDRA WALLACE

Frosted transparent beads in pale pink, pale mauve and white are used to stunning effect in this amulet purse. The frosted beads have a misty appearance and the colours are reminiscent of dawn. Larger frosted beads edge the fringe and also decorate the strap.

Pale blue-grey 60%

Amethyst 10%

Blue 15%

Grey pearls 15%

Frosted white 30%

Frosted pink 30%

Frosted mauve 40%

WINTER MORNING
TESSA HALFPENNY

This is a beautiful necklace in grey and lavender. The base is made from right-angle weave in triangle beads, which is embellished with seed beads. A large floral focal bead is attached with a narrow chain so that it hangs in front of the necklace. This grey-lavender colour scheme is reminiscent of wintery dawn mornings.

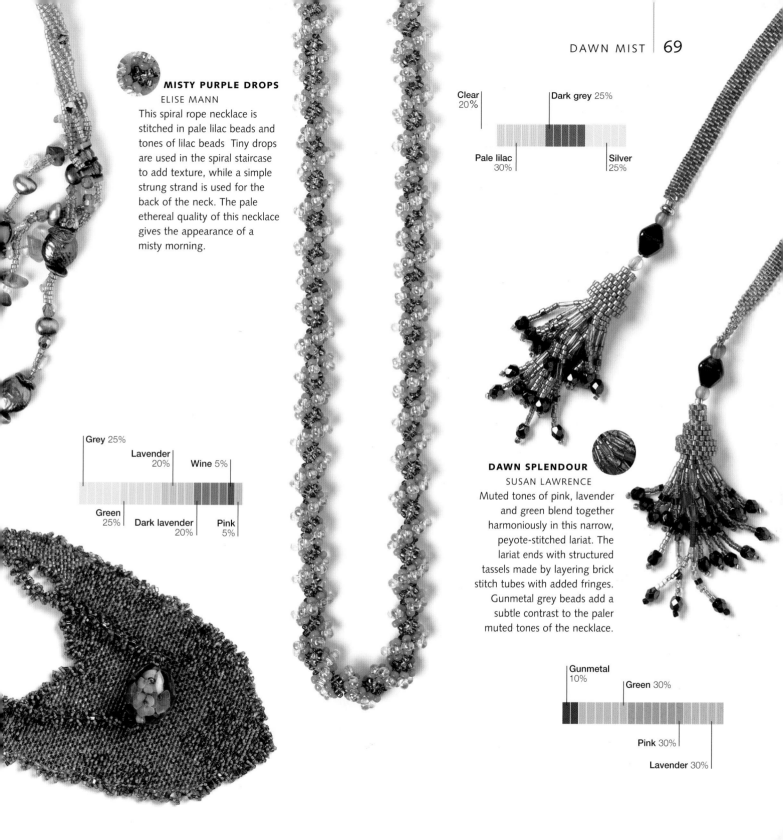

MISTY PURPLE DROPS
ELISE MANN

This spiral rope necklace is stitched in pale lilac beads and tones of lilac beads Tiny drops are used in the spiral staircase to add texture, while a simple strung strand is used for the back of the neck. The pale ethereal quality of this necklace gives the appearance of a misty morning.

Clear 20% | Dark grey 25%
Pale lilac 30% | Silver 25%

Grey 25%
Lavender 20%
Wine 5%
Green 25%
Dark lavender 20%
Pink 5%

DAWN SPLENDOUR
SUSAN LAWRENCE

Muted tones of pink, lavender and green blend together harmoniously in this narrow, peyote-stitched lariat. The lariat ends with structured tassels made by layering brick stitch tubes with added fringes. Gunmetal grey beads add a subtle contrast to the paler muted tones of the necklace.

Gunmetal 10%
Green 30%
Pink 30%
Lavender 30%

Faded roses

THE SOFT AND GENTLE COLOURS OF DRIED ROSES HAVE A SUBTLE AND ROMANTIC BEAUTY.

These colour schemes of muted ambers, browns and pinks often have a vintage look to them. Here you will find an analogous colour scheme of muted yellow, orange and red, contrasted with shades of green, with colours ranging from dark and moody to soft and feminine.

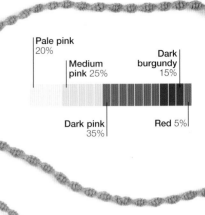

Pale pink 20%

Medium pink 25%

Dark burgundy 15%

Dark pink 35%

Red 5%

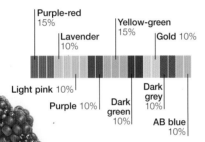

Purple-red 15%

Lavender 10%

Yellow-green 15%

Gold 10%

Light pink 10%

Purple 10%

Dark green 10%

Dark grey 10%

AB blue 10%

RUSSIAN HOLIDAY
BAR BLAKEY

A varied selection of beaded beads in complementary colours have been strung on a braided cord to make this necklace. Each bead is different, producing textural interest. The colours in the cord mirror the colours of the beads, so that they blend together perfectly.

SPICY SPIRAL
BAR BLAKEY

The beauty of this necklace lies in the simplicity of its design. This beaded rope can be worn in a variety of ways and will suit a range of colour schemes. The more muted shades of brown, green and lilac are given a boost by the brighter pink.

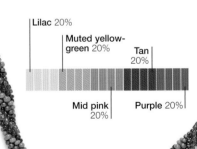

Lilac 20%

Muted yellow-green 20%

Tan 20%

Mid pink 20%

Purple 20%

FIBRE AND BEAD NECKLACE
JANE OLSEN-PHILLIPS

There are beautiful tonal variations in this woven necklace The monochromatic colour scheme uses several shades of pink cord alongside beads in various shades and finishes of pink. A few Aurora Borealis (AB) coated beads sparkle in the fringe.

NETTED AMULET PURSE
ANNE CLARKE

This netted amulet purse is very elegantly stitched in muted brown-green seed beads with accents of gold-lined beads. Muted mauve tones in the fringe and strap are reminiscent of the colours of faded roses. There is a lovely sparkle to the strap and fringe and tiny roses are added for decoration.

Brown-green 35%
Muted gold 20%
Red-brown 30%
Muted mauve 15%

WIRED CUFF
JANE SADGROVE

A beautiful selection of beads has been used in this wire cuff, in various hues resembling faded roses. The touch of green and cream beads adds interest to this analogous colour scheme. The use of three colours of wire echoes the colours in the beads and integrates well into the overall colour scheme.

Green 5%
Amber 5%
Pale peach 30%
Rose pink 25%
Raspberry 30%
Cream 5%

Moorland heather

BE INSPIRED BY THE CHANGING SEASONS OF THE MOORLAND LANDSCAPE.

Moorland continually changes colour throughout the year, from yellow gorse and bright red-purple heather in summer to the more muted tones of green, brown, purple and red seen in the autumn and winter. The beadwork featured here endeavours to show how beautiful these muted tones can be.

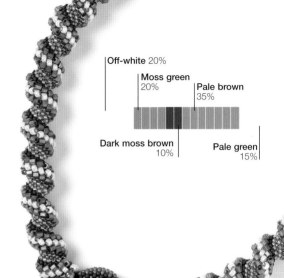

Off-white 20%

Moss green 20%

Pale brown 35%

Dark moss brown 10%

Pale green 15%

MAGIC CARPET
JENNY BOYLE

Tones of red, blue and mauve are set against an earth tone background. These subtle shades have a delicate beauty, are gentle, and blend well with most dark and neutral colours. There is an old, faded quality to this spectacle case, which is reinforced by the antique gold beads.

Antique brown 30%

Blue 15%

Beige 15%

Red 5%

Yellow-beige 5%

AB mauve 10%

Gold 20%

ORINOCO
J. WOOD

Right-angle weave has been used in a freeform technique for this unique necklace. The muted greens and red-purple are indicative of the landscape. The shading from one colour to the next is quite subtle and the larger beads and spaces add discreet texture to this piece.

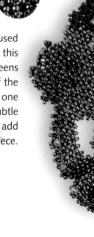

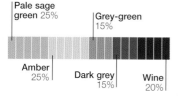

SEA STORM TWIST
HEATHER FENN-EDWARDS

Mossy green and brown have been used in this spiral, with tones ranging from pale to dark. The twisted peyote spiral is the perfect complement to the focal point, a stone held in place with peyote beadwork. This colour scheme reflects the changing colours of moorland heath.

Pale sage green 25%
Grey-green 15%
Amber 25%
Dark grey 15%
Wine 20%

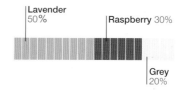

BUTTON PENDANT
STEPHNEY HORNBLOW

The subtle shading of lavender and red is reminiscent of moorland heather with a beautiful sunset. The colours are subtly blended in the herringbone rope, with more distinction in the pendant. The use of buttons is an interesting design feature.

Lavender 50%
Raspberry 30%
Grey 20%

ROCK CANDY
C. LAVIN

The glass beads in this necklace encompass all the colours of moorland: the purple heather, the bright green of early summer and the burnt orange and red of autumn. These beads have an attractive surface texture and the variation of colour within the beads is wonderful.

Green 10%
Red-brown 10%
Sea green 10%
Pale lavender 10%
Yellow-green 15%
Dark amber 15%
Apricot 10%
Purple 10%
Pink-red 10%

Carnival colours

INDULGE YOURSELF IN A CELEBRATION OF COLOUR!

The word 'carnival' conjures up images of bright, daring schemes. Bright colours don't always have to appear garish, but to look good, they do need to be used in the correct proportions, finishes and tones. The examples shown here demonstrate the range of bright colour schemes, from sophistication to fantasy to fun.

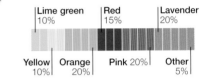

Lime green 10%		Red 15%		Lavender 20%
Yellow 10%	Orange 20%		Pink 20%	Other 5%

PINK PARADE
SANDRA WALLACE

The six colours featured in this necklace are all cool, including the lemon and pink. The biggest proportions are blues, purple and pink, with contrasting complementary colours of lemon and lime. This necklace shows that bright does not have to be primary. The butterfly-netting technique creates a speckled effect.

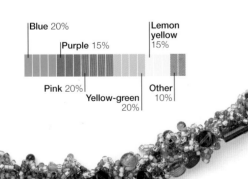

Blue 20%			Lemon yellow 15%
Purple 15%			
Pink 20%	Yellow-green 20%		Other 10%

MARDI GRAS AT NIGHT
ELISE MANN

A stunning bracelet, reflecting the lights of the carnival at night, provides great inspiration for the faint-hearted. It is a fabulous mixture of luminous beads set against black. Black tends to make colours appear brighter but, in this case, the black cord emphasizes the luminosity of the beads without them appearing too gaudy.

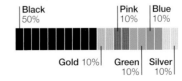

Black 50%		Pink 10%	Blue 10%
	Gold 10%	Green 10%	Silver 10%

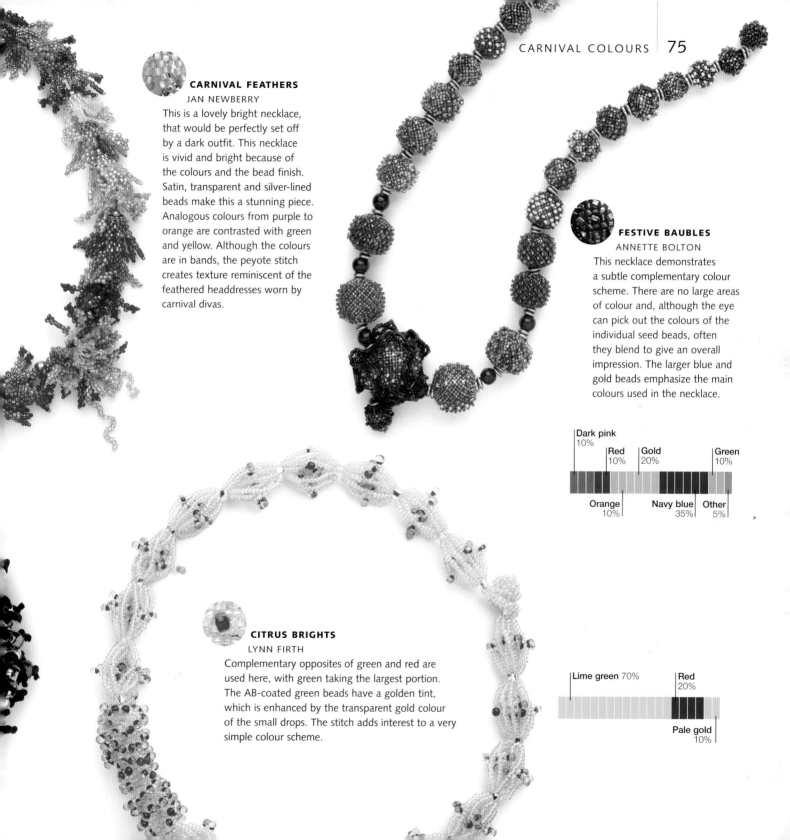

CARNIVAL FEATHERS
JAN NEWBERRY

This is a lovely bright necklace, that would be perfectly set off by a dark outfit. This necklace is vivid and bright because of the colours and the bead finish. Satin, transparent and silver-lined beads make this a stunning piece. Analogous colours from purple to orange are contrasted with green and yellow. Although the colours are in bands, the peyote stitch creates texture reminiscent of the feathered headdresses worn by carnival divas.

FESTIVE BAUBLES
ANNETTE BOLTON

This necklace demonstrates a subtle complementary colour scheme. There are no large areas of colour and, although the eye can pick out the colours of the individual seed beads, often they blend to give an overall impression. The larger blue and gold beads emphasize the main colours used in the necklace.

Dark pink 10%
Red 10%
Gold 20%
Green 10%
Orange 10%
Navy blue 35%
Other 5%

CITRUS BRIGHTS
LYNN FIRTH

Complementary opposites of green and red are used here, with green taking the largest portion. The AB-coated green beads have a golden tint, which is enhanced by the transparent gold colour of the small drops. The stitch adds interest to a very simple colour scheme.

Lime green 70%
Red 20%
Pale gold 10%

World inspirations

LOOK TO OTHER COUNTRIES AND CULTURES FOR INSPIRATION.

Nearly all cultures and countries from around the world have traditional jewellery. However, the variety of bead finishes available today means that beadwork and jewellery have evolved. Here we have a mixture of bold and colourful designs, both traditional and modern, inspired by cultures from all around the world.

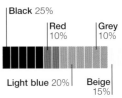

TEENAGE DREAM
KATI TORDA

The focal point of this African necklace is the carved bone centrepiece. The orange and blue complementary colours stand out against the black on the strung sections. There is a great deal of texture in this necklace, with the wired beads attached like charms either side of the centrepiece.

AFRICAN MASK
CLAIRE CROUCHLEY

The black beadwork is the perfect background for the vivid orange and red geometric shapes in this symbolic design. The touch of blue and green adds that final spark of interest. The design is followed through into the fringe with its vibrant colours and lovely shape.

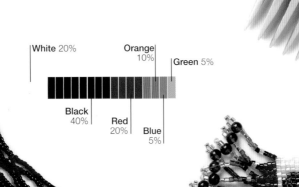

White 20%   Orange 10%   Green 5%

Black 40%   Red 20%   Blue 5%

Black 25%   Red 10%   Grey 10%   Orange 10%

Light blue 20%   Beige 15%   Grey metal 10%

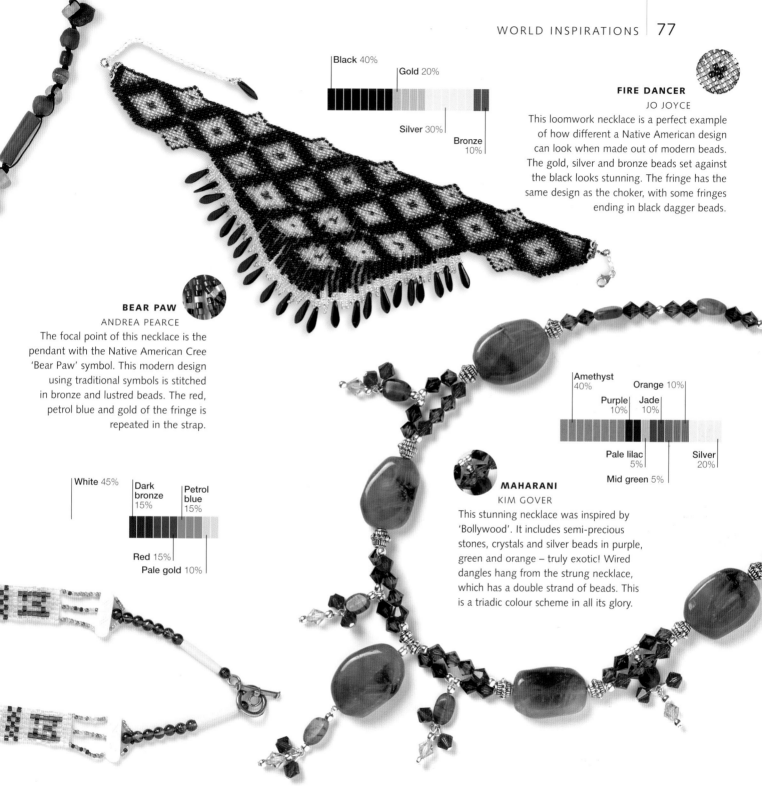

Black 40%
Gold 20%
Silver 30%
Bronze 10%

FIRE DANCER
JO JOYCE

This loomwork necklace is a perfect example of how different a Native American design can look when made out of modern beads. The gold, silver and bronze beads set against the black looks stunning. The fringe has the same design as the choker, with some fringes ending in black dagger beads.

BEAR PAW
ANDREA PEARCE

The focal point of this necklace is the pendant with the Native American Cree 'Bear Paw' symbol. This modern design using traditional symbols is stitched in bronze and lustred beads. The red, petrol blue and gold of the fringe is repeated in the strap.

White 45%
Dark bronze 15%
Petrol blue 15%
Red 15%
Pale gold 10%

Amethyst 40%
Orange 10%
Purple 10%
Jade 10%
Pale lilac 5%
Silver 20%
Mid green 5%

MAHARANI
KIM GOVER

This stunning necklace was inspired by 'Bollywood'. It includes semi-precious stones, crystals and silver beads in purple, green and orange – truly exotic! Wired dangles hang from the strung necklace, which has a double strand of beads. This is a triadic colour scheme in all its glory.

The magic of magenta

MAGENTA, CERISE OR FUCHSIA — WHATEVER YOU CALL THIS COLOUR — HAS A MAGICAL QUALITY.

Magenta cannot fail to be noticed. It is stunning with black, contrasts well with its near complement of lime green, looks lovely with turquoise and brightens up purple. The wonderful array of beadwork here shows how this colour can be used in a variety of projects, so explore the many possibilities.

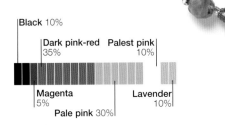

COCKTAIL CUFF
HEATHER FENN-EDWARDS
Various shades of magenta and pink are used in this exquisite bracelet. The paler pinks slightly tone down the overall brightness, but the black accent beads add excitement to the overall scheme. The variety of beads in this bracelet add a wonderful textural quality to this freeform technique.

Black 10%
Dark pink-red 35%   Palest pink 10%

Magenta 5%   Lavender 10%
Pale pink 30%

TURKISH DELIGHT
HEATHER FENN-EDWARDS
This is an excellent example of a complementary colour scheme in red-purple and yellow-green. The colours flow around the plaited herringbone rope with lovely tonal variations. The focal point is the mask, which is outlined with freeform peyote, where a variety of sizes and colours of bead have been used.

PEARL BLUE
PIPPA LUDLOW
Set magenta against turquoise for a wonderful vibrancy. The dyed pearls have a luminosity that is matched by the shiny seed beads. This is a great colour scheme where the magenta pearls take centre stage by virtue of their size and the fact that red tones advance whereas blue tones recede.

Terracotta 5%
Purple 15%
Pale green 20%   Red 5%
Turquoise 10%

Green 20%   Cerise 10%
Pale lavender 15%

MAGIC CARPET
C. LAVIN

The cerise paired with dark red-purple makes a bright but not dazzling piece of jewellery. Black, silver and transparent beads add a subtle variation to this stylish strung necklace, which has wirework drops flowing around the neck.

Black 5%
Gold 10%
Cerise 25%
Pink 35%
Dark cerise 15%
Mid cerise 10%

Black 30%
Cerise 20%
Pink cerise 50%

MOULIN ROUGE
ELAINE PEEL

The cerise and black colour scheme makes this tassel truly stunning. It beautifully demonstrates how vibrant cerise can be. Here, the different techniques flow from one to the next to make a uniform design until you reach the skirt. Then there is a wonderful undulating frill that is dripping with crystals.

Turquoise 75%
Magenta 25%

Stained glass windows

USE A SPECTRUM OF COLOURS TOGETHER IN A SINGLE PIECE OF JEWELLERY.

We all love to gaze at stained glass windows; the colours are so vivid with the light shining through them. Some multi-coloured bead schemes can be clashing, while others retain a certain uniformity. These pieces of jewellery will certainly command attention and should be worn against a plain background.

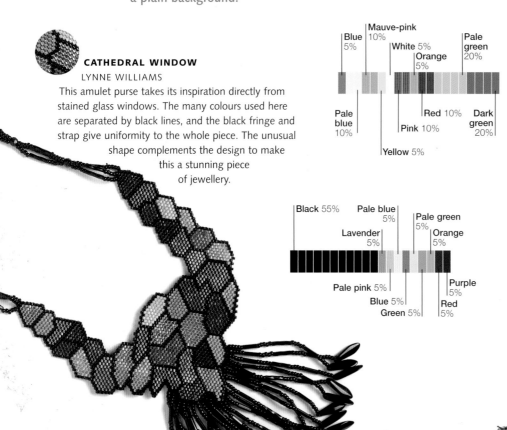

CATHEDRAL WINDOW
LYNNE WILLIAMS
This amulet purse takes its inspiration directly from stained glass windows. The many colours used here are separated by black lines, and the black fringe and strap give uniformity to the whole piece. The unusual shape complements the design to make this a stunning piece of jewellery.

Blue 5%
Mauve-pink 10%
White 5%
Orange 5%
Pale green 20%
Pale blue 10%
Red 10%
Dark green 20%
Pink 10%
Yellow 5%

Black 55%
Pale blue 5%
Lavender 5%
Pale green 5%
Orange 5%
Pale pink 5%
Purple 5%
Blue 5%
Red 5%
Green 5%

THE BLACK WIDOW'S GARDEN
J. WOOD
Red, orange and yellow are the dominant colours in this piece. The many shades of green and blue form a subtle background for the bright colours. The pink flowers almost clash with the bright colours, but because the yellow and red are so dominant they remain in the background.

Black 20%
Blue 10%
Bright yellow 10%
Green 10%
Purple-pink 10%

Red 10%
Turquoise 10%
White 10%

Dark red 10%

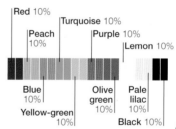

AFRICAN NECKLACE
MONICA BOXLEY

This colourful necklace is made with glass trading beads originally from the Czech Republic and exchanged with people in West Africa over the past 300 years. It has every colour of the rainbow, some with tints and shades, thus varying the tone. However, the red and yellow beads will advance because they are warm colours.

Red 10%
Peach 10%
Turquoise 10%
Purple 10%
Lemon 10%

Blue 10%
Olive green 10%
Pale lilac 10%

Yellow-green 10%
Black 10%

FRINGED CUFF
HEATHER KINGSLEY-HEATH

An analogous colour scheme of red and pale mauve with a touch of blue makes this a slightly clashing mix of colours. This daring colour scheme is reserved for those who love bold statements. The frills and fringes create wonderful textural interest in this cuff.

Red 40%
Pale blue 15%

Pale mauve 35%
Purple 10%

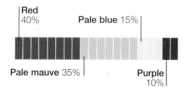

PATCHWORK PURSE
ISOBELLE BUNTING

The colour scheme in this purse contains all three primary and all three secondary colours of the colour wheel. The palest tints of yellow and lilac allow the red and bright blue to dominate. This colour scheme works well because of the variation in tonal value and the proportions of the colours used.

Lavender fields

LAVENDER HUES HAVE AN ATTRACTIVENESS THAT IS
CALM AND SOOTHING.

The phrase 'lavender fields' evokes images of pale purple flowers
and calming fragrances. The purple fields seem to go on forever,
and all the eye can see is a sea of lavender hues. If you love
lavender, then there is a colour scheme here for you, from bright to
muted, pale to dark.

ALL HEART
ELAINE PEEL
Beautiful sculptural beadwork surrounds
this abalone shell. Light to dark green
and tones of lavender reflect the colours
seen in the shell. This attractive heart-
shaped brooch is given texture by the
freeform peyote stitch that surrounds it.

PEIROT
ELAINE PEEL
The purple hues in this analogous
colour scheme range from blue-purple
to red-purple. The diamond shapes in
the geometric design are outlined with
gold, which adds a wonderful richness.
The skirt is enhanced with a sequence
of linked diamonds and the head is
further embellished with gold.

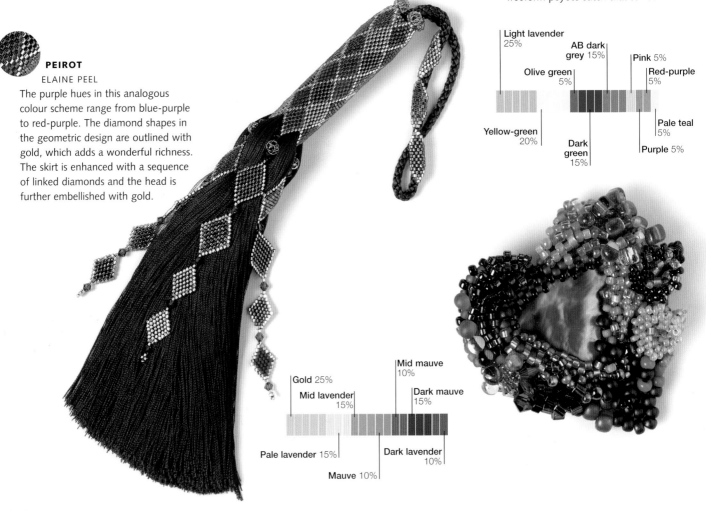

Light lavender 25%
AB dark grey 15%
Pink 5%
Red-purple 5%
Olive green 5%
Yellow-green 20%
Dark green 15%
Pale teal 5%
Purple 5%

Gold 25%
Mid lavender 15%
Mid mauve 10%
Dark mauve 15%
Pale lavender 15%
Dark lavender 10%
Mauve 10%

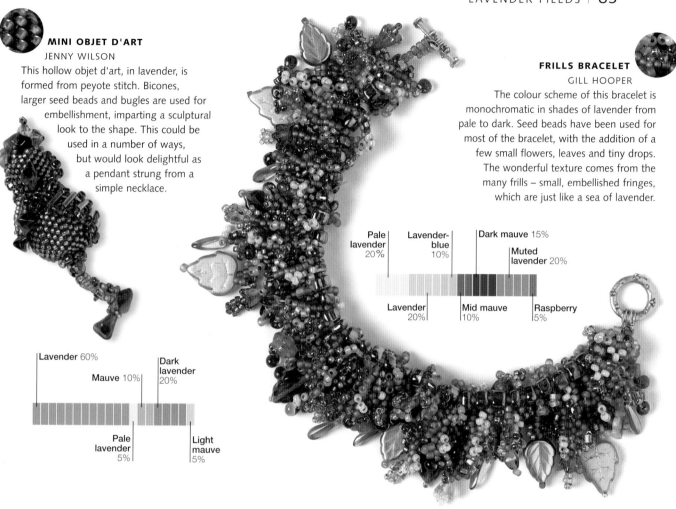

MINI OBJET D'ART
JENNY WILSON

This hollow objet d'art, in lavender, is formed from peyote stitch. Bicones, larger seed beads and bugles are used for embellishment, imparting a sculptural look to the shape. This could be used in a number of ways, but would look delightful as a pendant strung from a simple necklace.

FRILLS BRACELET
GILL HOOPER

The colour scheme of this bracelet is monochromatic in shades of lavender from pale to dark. Seed beads have been used for most of the bracelet, with the addition of a few small flowers, leaves and tiny drops. The wonderful texture comes from the many frills – small, embellished fringes, which are just like a sea of lavender.

Pale lavender 20%
Lavender-blue 10%
Dark mauve 15%
Muted lavender 20%
Lavender 20%
Mid mauve 10%
Raspberry 5%

Lavender 60%
Mauve 10%
Dark lavender 20%
Pale lavender 5%
Light mauve 5%

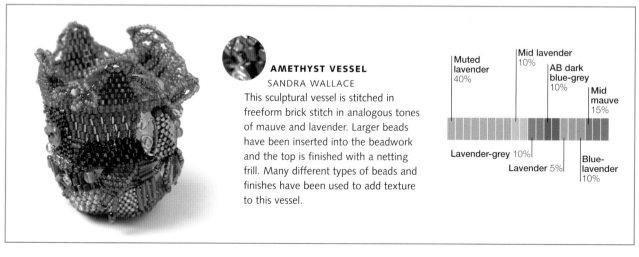

AMETHYST VESSEL
SANDRA WALLACE

This sculptural vessel is stitched in freeform brick stitch in analogous tones of mauve and lavender. Larger beads have been inserted into the beadwork and the top is finished with a netting frill. Many different types of beads and finishes have been used to add texture to this vessel.

Muted lavender 40%
Mid lavender 10%
AB dark blue-grey 10%
Mid mauve 15%
Lavender-grey 10%
Lavender 5%
Blue-lavender 10%

Rose garden

A ROSE GARDEN BRINGS TO MIND ROMANTIC COLOURS AND SCENTS.

Although roses are available in most colours, this theme concentrates on the charming pink colour schemes. Pink, used with lilac, gives an analogous colour scheme that is soft and gentle. Green is a good complementary background colour for pink, while yellow-green will create an almost clashing yet interesting colour scheme.

DOG ROSE
LYNNE FIRTH

This perfect example of a dog rose is so realistic that you could almost believe it was picked from the hedgerow. It is stitched in delicate pink and white with soft dark-green leaves and a yellow centre. The edges have been softened by adding small stitched flowers.

Pale pink 15%
Pale green 25%
White 5%
Palest pink 20%
Dark green 30%
Yellow 5%

HERRINGBONE NECKLACE
ISOBELLE BUNTING

This necklace takes its colour scheme from the wonderful lime green and pink lampwork beads. Sections of herringbone rope in matching colours have been strung between the beads. The simple stitch and the plain colour of the rope complements the glass beads.

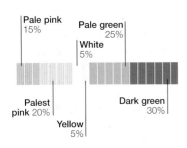

PRETTY IN PINK
GILL HOOPER

This Dutch spiral bracelet with colours ranging from pale to dark raspberry pink follows a monochromatic colour scheme. A variety of beads have been used to create texture, including square beads and different-sized seed beads.

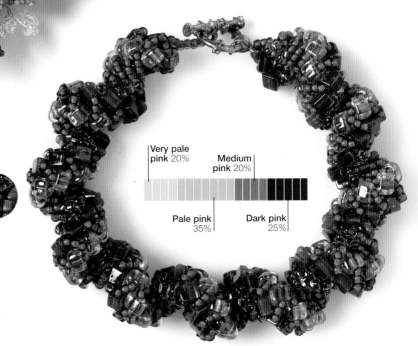

Very pale pink 20%
Medium pink 20%
Pale pink 35%
Dark pink 25%

Very dark pink
15%

Lime
green
70%

Clear
15%

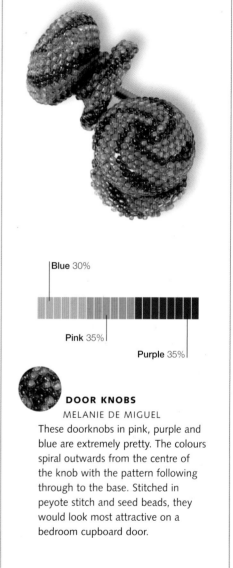

Blue 30%

Pink 35%

Purple 35%

ROSE TRELLIS
JAN NEWBERRY

This pretty pendant has pink flowers scattered on a netted background, giving the appearance of flowers on a trellis. The design uses a slightly clashing colour scheme of pink and yellow-green – several shades of pink provide variation and depth of colour.

DOOR KNOBS
MELANIE DE MIGUEL

These doorknobs in pink, purple and blue are extremely pretty. The colours spiral outwards from the centre of the knob with the pattern following through to the base. Stitched in peyote stitch and seed beads, they would look most attractive on a bedroom cupboard door.

Pale pink
20%

Medium pink
20%

Dark pink
30%

Yellow-green
30%

Arctic winter

NOTHING COMPARES TO THE CLEAN FRESH
LOOK OF ICE AND SNOW.

The beadwork displayed here shows frozen water
in all its glory, with schemes ranging from clear
colourless crystals to pale blue and green. The
jewellery on these pages would add a touch of
sparkle to any occasion.

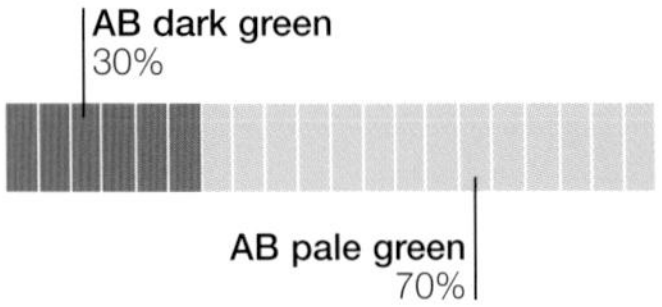

AB dark green
30%

AB pale green
70%

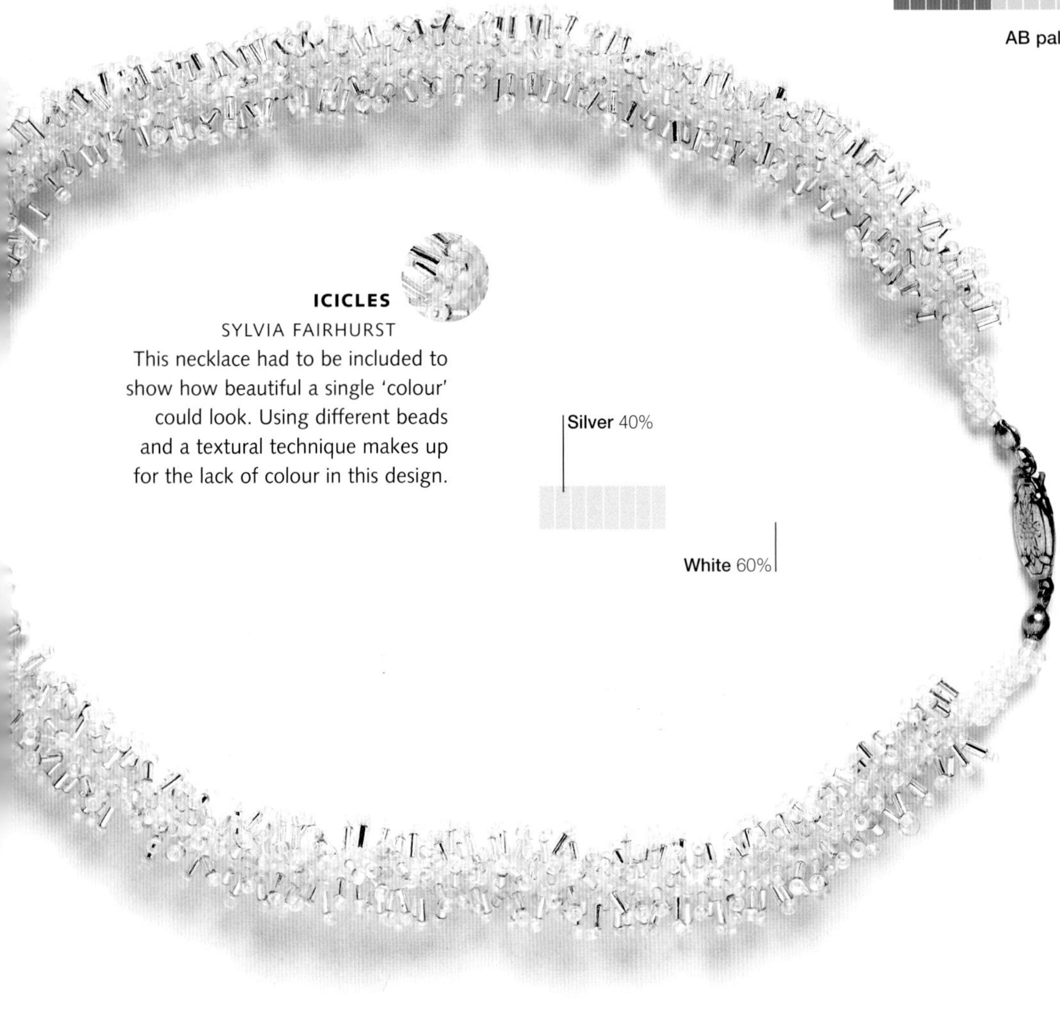

ICICLES
SYLVIA FAIRHURST
This necklace had to be included to
show how beautiful a single 'colour'
could look. Using different beads
and a textural technique makes up
for the lack of colour in this design.

Silver 40%

White 60%

ICY FERNS
MARGE QUINN
The transparent and pale green
beads, both with an Aurora Borealis
(AB) finish, give an icy feel to this
necklace. The feathery branched
fringes add a focal point, while the
icy colour looks like early morning
frost. The small picots on the ladder-
stitched strand add interest to this
delicate design.

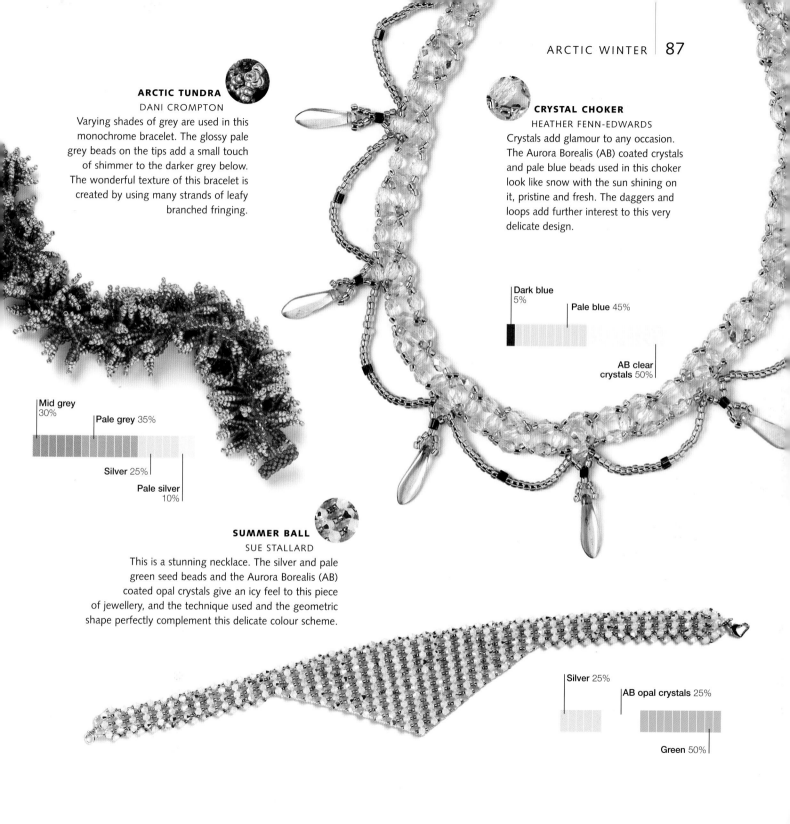

ARCTIC TUNDRA
DANI CROMPTON
Varying shades of grey are used in this monochrome bracelet. The glossy pale grey beads on the tips add a small touch of shimmer to the darker grey below. The wonderful texture of this bracelet is created by using many strands of leafy branched fringing.

CRYSTAL CHOKER
HEATHER FENN-EDWARDS
Crystals add glamour to any occasion. The Aurora Borealis (AB) coated crystals and pale blue beads used in this choker look like snow with the sun shining on it, pristine and fresh. The daggers and loops add further interest to this very delicate design.

Dark blue 5%
Pale blue 45%
AB clear crystals 50%

Mid grey 30%
Pale grey 35%
Silver 25%
Pale silver 10%

SUMMER BALL
SUE STALLARD
This is a stunning necklace. The silver and pale green seed beads and the Aurora Borealis (AB) coated opal crystals give an icy feel to this piece of jewellery, and the technique used and the geometric shape perfectly complement this delicate colour scheme.

Silver 25%
AB opal crystals 25%
Green 50%

Springtime

THE FIRST GLIMMERS OF SPRING LIFT THE
EMOTIONS AFTER THE DREARY DAYS OF WINTER.

Fresh green shoots are seen pushing out of the barren
soil, and lilac and yellow flowers abound in spring.
Everything has a clean, fresh feel to it, and the season
prescribes light and bright colours. The colours of
spring are clear and not muted, for example the green
of spring is a fresh true green.

SPRING GREEN
SANDRA WALLACE

Lime green- and lilac-coloured cube beads are
stitched in herringbone and brick stitch for this
striped bracelet. The herringbone stitch gives
a smooth fabric, which is flexible. The bracelet
is embellished with a dainty spring-like flower,
which is also worked in herringbone stitch.

HYDRANGEA
SANDRA WALLACE

The inspiration behind this split
loom necklace is the colour of
hydrangeas. However, it is very
'spring-like' in colour: fresh green
contrasts with pink, raspberry
and lavender, while the touch of
pale aqua gives a lovely cool and
fresh look. The geometric shape
is softened by the long fringe and
strung warps.

Lilac 60%

Lime green 40%

Lavender 20%

Raspberry 10%

Fresh green 10%

Aqua 5%

Pale pink 15%

Lime green 10%

Pale aqua 15%

Silver 15%

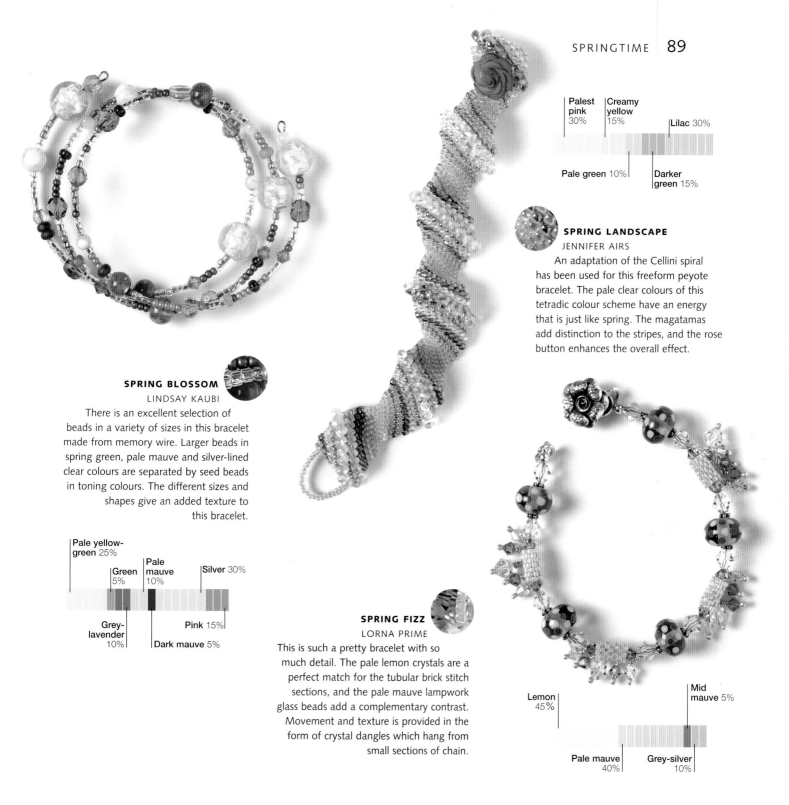

Palest pink 30% **Creamy yellow** 15% **Lilac** 30%

Pale green 10% **Darker green** 15%

SPRING LANDSCAPE
JENNIFER AIRS
An adaptation of the Cellini spiral has been used for this freeform peyote bracelet. The pale clear colours of this tetradic colour scheme have an energy that is just like spring. The magatamas add distinction to the stripes, and the rose button enhances the overall effect.

SPRING BLOSSOM
LINDSAY KAUBI
There is an excellent selection of beads in a variety of sizes in this bracelet made from memory wire. Larger beads in spring green, pale mauve and silver-lined clear colours are separated by seed beads in toning colours. The different sizes and shapes give an added texture to this bracelet.

Pale yellow-green 25%
Green 5%
Pale mauve 10%
Silver 30%
Grey-lavender 10%
Pink 15%
Dark mauve 5%

SPRING FIZZ
LORNA PRIME
This is such a pretty bracelet with so much detail. The pale lemon crystals are a perfect match for the tubular brick stitch sections, and the pale mauve lampwork glass beads add a complementary contrast. Movement and texture is provided in the form of crystal dangles which hang from small sections of chain.

Lemon 45%
Mid mauve 5%
Pale mauve 40%
Grey-silver 10%

Citus

CITRUS COLOURS ARE ACIDIC AND VIBRANT, BUT CAN BE SOFTENED.

These analogous citrus colour schemes are fresh and sharp, giving vitality to any item. If you want a less vivid but still lively effect, adding white to these colours will make softer sherbet colours. Here are a variety of ways of using citrus colours, some more vibrant than others.

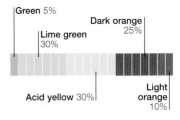

CITRUS ZEST
SANDRA WALLACE

This analogous colour scheme is brought to life with vivid lime green, acid yellow and bright orange. The freeform peyote stitch blends the colours in such a way that you see all of them, without any one colour being too dominant.

SHERBET DIP
SANDRA WALLACE

These young, fashionable colours are more gentle than pure citrus colours, yet they still retain a fresh, sharp feel to them. The tangerine, lemon, pink and soft green of the polymer clay beads are echoed in the spiral rope. Taking your colour scheme from a set of handmade beads is an ideal way to create consistency in your beadwork.

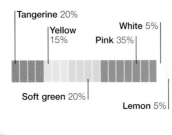

Tangerine 20%
Yellow 15%
White 5%
Pink 35%
Soft green 20%
Lemon 5%

Green 5%
Dark orange 25%
Lime green 30%
Acid yellow 30%
Light orange 10%

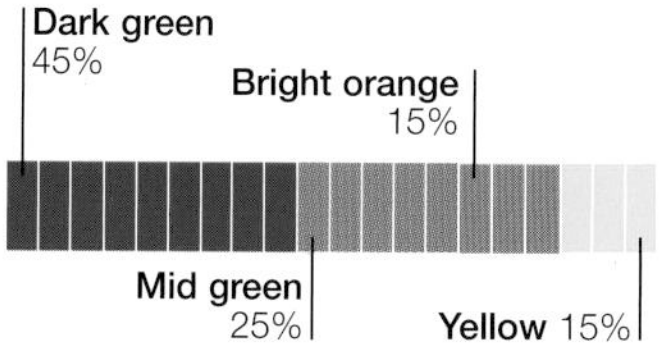

Dark green
45%

Bright orange
15%

Mid green
25%

Yellow 15%

ORCHARD FRUITS
SANDRA WALLACE

These earrings use brightly coloured glass oranges and lemons, which are offset by the dark green leaves. These fun citrus earrings are made using a simple branched fringe, but consider making a spiral where orange and yellow stripes are set against a dark green background. That would be stunning!

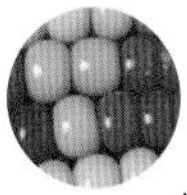

Pale yellow
85%

Orange
15%

CARNIVAL BROOCH
HEATHER KINGSLEY-HEATH

Bright orange and bright green are a bold combination of colours that are vivid and almost clashing. These two colours have nearly the same tonal value, but they are not quite as contrasting as red and green would be. It is still a colour scheme that is definitely not for the faint-hearted!

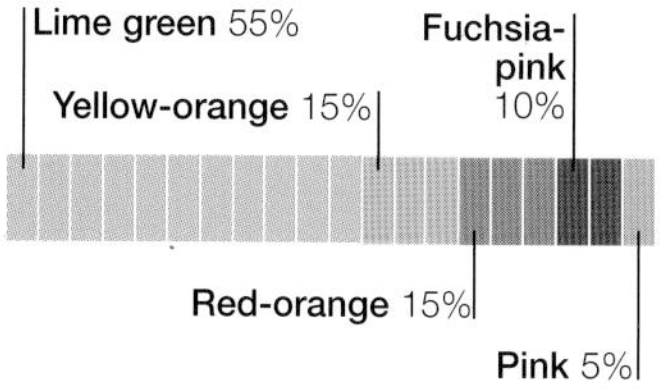

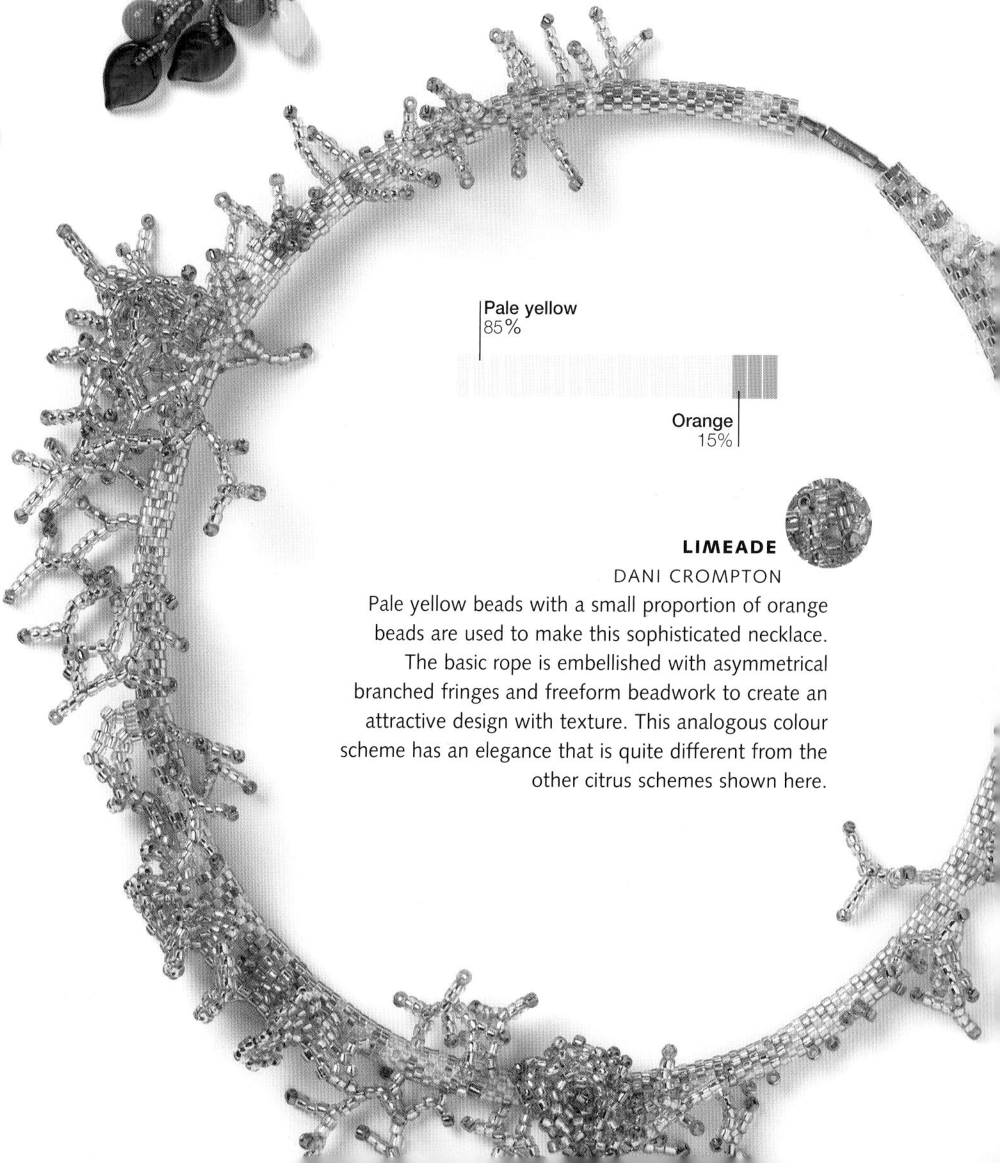

LIMEADE
DANI CROMPTON

Pale yellow beads with a small proportion of orange beads are used to make this sophisticated necklace. The basic rope is embellished with asymmetrical branched fringes and freeform beadwork to create an attractive design with texture. This analogous colour scheme has an elegance that is quite different from the other citrus schemes shown here.

Lime green 55%

Fuchsia-
pink
10%

Yellow-orange 15%

Red-orange 15%

Pink 5%

Golden glamour

GOLD BRINGS TO MIND OPULENCE, PROSPERITY AND RICHES.

Gold is warm toned and goes well with warm colours, but can also look good with blue and green, depending on the hue. Used with discretion it is very elegant, but too much gold can be overwhelming. Bronze is a good alternative to using gold in beadwork, as it tones down the glitzy effect.

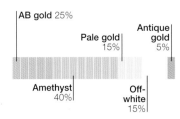

BRONZE CHOKER
MARGE QUINN

Two different types of bronze beads have been used in this delicate choker. The bugle beads in the centre add variation in texture and colour because of the way the light reflects on them. The dainty fringes contain crystal drops, which reflect the light and add sparkle to this charming choker.

AMETHYST GOLD
SANDRA WALLACE

Metallic Aurora Borealis (AB) coated gold beads form the background for this amulet purse which uses pale beige and off-white beads for the pattern. The delicate fringe incorporates amethyst bicone and antique gold puffed square beads. The three V-shaped fringes in the centre add an individual effect, which is very graceful.

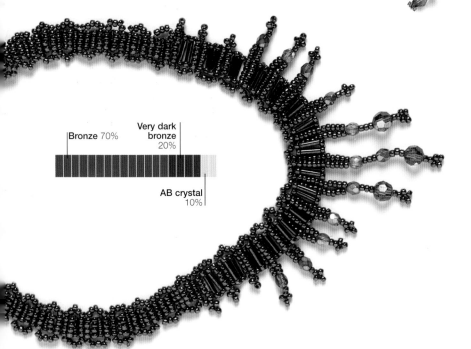

Bronze 70%
Very dark bronze 20%
AB crystal 10%

AB gold 25%
Pale gold 15%
Antique gold 5%
Amethyst 40%
Off-white 15%

CRYSTAL AMBER
ELISE MANN

This wonderful spiral staircase necklace is made from both gold and bronze seed beads and with crystals. The amber crystals catch the light from all directions, producing a lovely sparkle. The single strand of beads at the back of the neck makes it very comfortable to wear.

Bronze 40%   Amber 40%
Gold 20%

PEARLS, CRYSTALS, & GOLD
S. NEILSON

Pearls, crystals and gold are combined in this necklace to sophisticated effect. The variety of tones used in the pearls is echoed in the crystals, which creates unity. Shades of bronze, peach, beige and grey are interspersed with gold spacers to make a very elegant necklace.

Beige 40%   Peach 10%   Gold 10%
Grey 30%   Mid bronze 10%

ART DECO FAN BROOCH
MELANIE DE MIGUEL

Tones of bronze and gold are used for this elegant brooch. The herringbone fan shape is beautifully followed through into the fringe. There is a good use of different finishes of beads in the metallic and transparent seed beads and crystals.

Bronze 15%   Amber 15%
Gold 60%   White 10%

Midnight

BLACK IS CLASSIC, TIMELESS AND ALWAYS ELEGANT.

Black is perfect for a night out, and the pieces shown here will certainly enhance any outfit. The common theme with these items is understated elegance – they are sophisticated without being garish. Gold enriches and warms whereas silver gives a cool elegance.

| Black 50% | | | | | | Gunmetal 15% | | Steel 15% | | Galvanized crystal 5% | Silver 15% | |

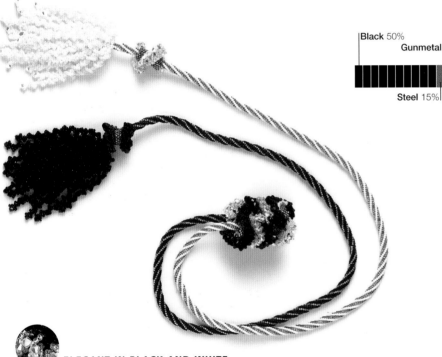

ELEGANT IN BLACK AND WHITE
SUE STALLARD

Black and white is smart and timeless. The proportions of black and white are equal in this design, which is superb in its simplicity. It is asymmetrical, black on one side and white on the other, joined in the centre by a striped connector that is full of texture.

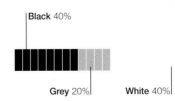

Black 40%

Grey 20%   White 40%

ART DECO
SANDRA WALLACE

In this formal, classic pendant the matt black beads show off the silver grey beads to perfection. Various tones of metallic beads have been used including gunmetal, silver and steel, together with galvanized crystal. A plain black strap and a simple fringe complement the effect.

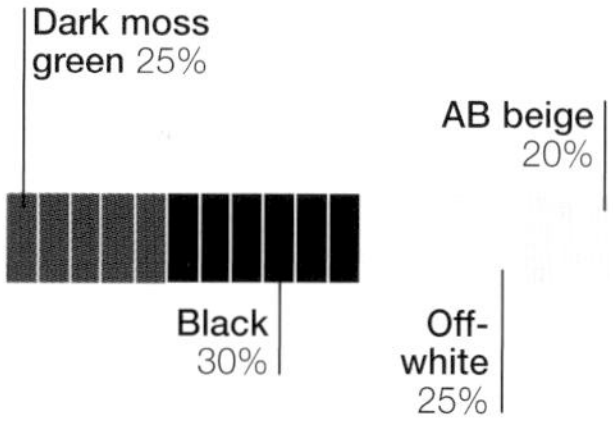

Dark moss green 25%

AB beige 20%

Black 30%

Off-white 25%

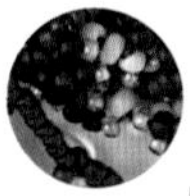

MIDNIGHT GARDEN
ISOBELLE BUNTING

The muted green in this necklace adds subtle variation to the spiral rope and is echoed in the leafy fringe. This is a well thought-out design, where the double rope is perfectly balanced by the texture of the leaves, producing beautiful asymmetry. The golden hue of the Aurora Borealis (AB) coating on the leaves enhances the overall colour scheme.

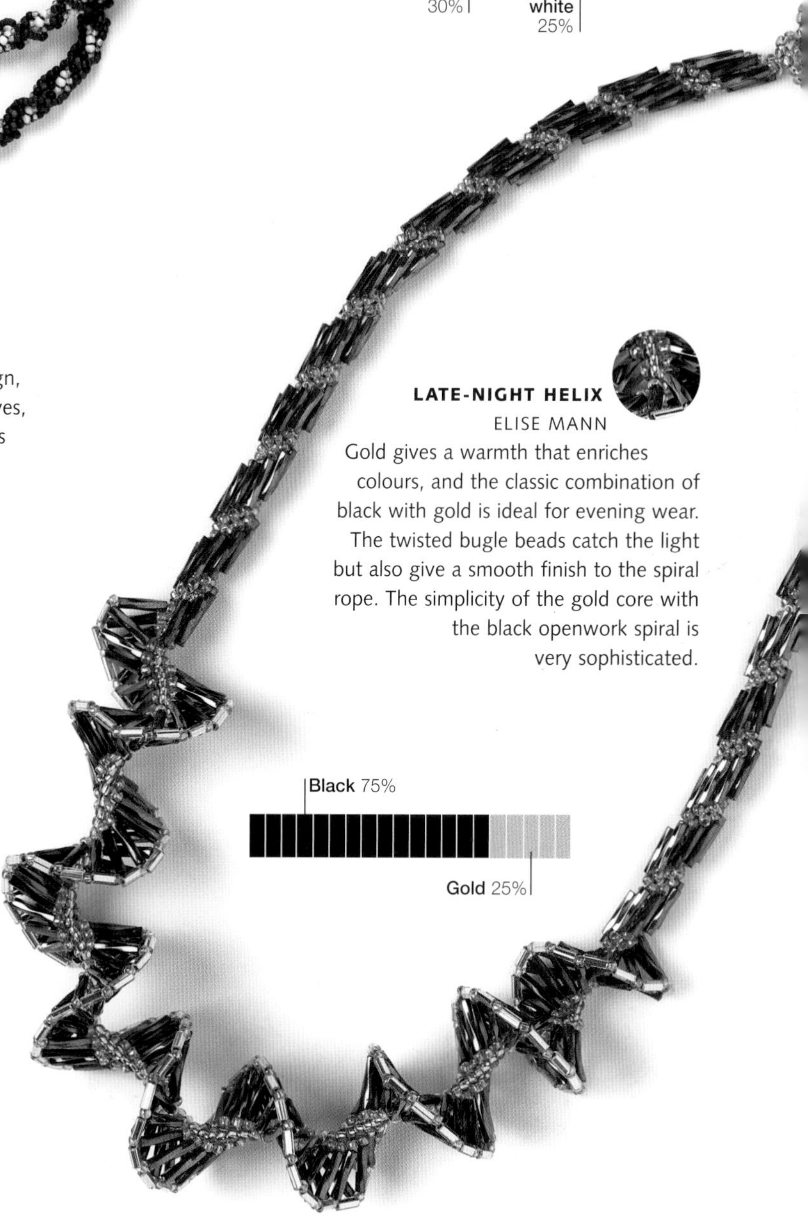

AB blue-grey 55%

Silver 45%

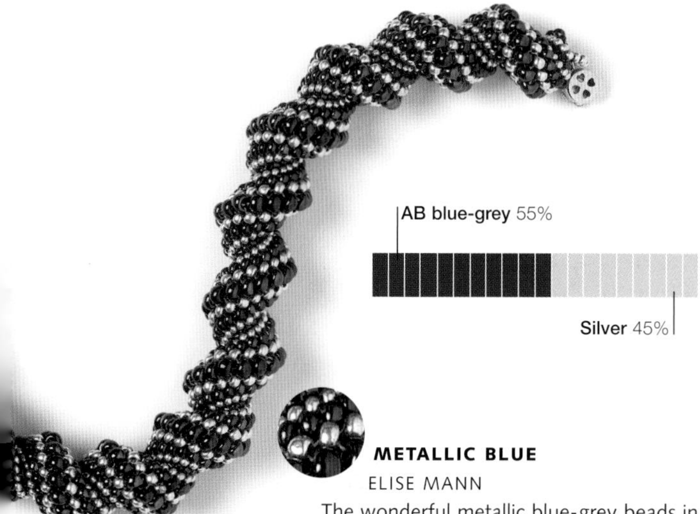

METALLIC BLUE
ELISE MANN

The wonderful metallic blue-grey beads in this bracelet will complement a variety of colour schemes. The gleam of the silver enhances the cool blue, while the peyote spiral creates visual interest in this cool two-tone colour scheme.

LATE-NIGHT HELIX
ELISE MANN

Gold gives a warmth that enriches colours, and the classic combination of black with gold is ideal for evening wear. The twisted bugle beads catch the light but also give a smooth finish to the spiral rope. The simplicity of the gold core with the black openwork spiral is very sophisticated.

Black 75%

Gold 25%

Regal splendour

REGAL SPLENDOUR BRINGS TO MIND THE RICH
COLOURS OF VELVET AND PRECIOUS JEWELS.

Ruby, emerald, sapphire and rich purple are colours
that have been associated with royalty for centuries.
Combine these colours with gold and they have a
refined and elegant beauty that is without comparison.

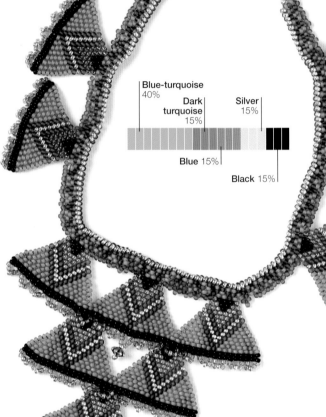

Blue-turquoise
40%
Dark
turquoise
15%
Silver
15%
Blue 15%
Black 15%

AB navy 40%
Mid purple
5%
Bronze
20%
Teal 15%
Pale aqua 15%
Lavender 5%

PEACOCK
LYNNE WILLIAMS
The grandeur of the peacock is often associated with
royalty. The beautiful peacock-eye feathers are made by
stitching around a pear-shaped bead with brick stitch.
The colours used mirror the iridescence of the peacock's
plumage and the bronze beads add contrast to this
analogous colour scheme.

EASTERN PROMISE
HEATHER FENN-EDWARDS
The triangular shapes in this
necklace bring to mind ancient
Egyptian images. Tones of
turquoise are enlivened with
silver and black seed beads,
which accentuate the symmetrical
design. Several finishes of bead
give depth to the turquoise, and a
lovely Venetian foiled-glass bead
is used to fasten the necklace.

CHANDELIER EARRINGS
LINDSAY KAUBI
The fire-polished crystals and silver make these extremely stylish earrings. Turquoise and ruby are rich colours, which always appear elegant. The beads are threaded on headpins and a mixture of seed beads and crystals give diversity to the strands.

Turquoise 40%

Mid blue 15%

Ruby 5%

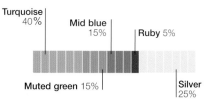

Muted green 15%

Silver 25%

AB teal 20%

Burgundy 20%

Green 10%

Red 5%

Bronze 20%

Dark purple 20%

Navy 5%

VENETIAN VESSEL
SANDRA WALLACE
This wirework vessel is made on a beading loom in sections. A wide variety of sizes and shapes of beads have been selected, giving this vessel a beautiful texture. Although all the colours of the rainbow have been used, most of the beads are rich and not vivid so the colours do not clash.

AB purple 33%

Gold 33%

Royal blue 34%

SPIRAL ROPE NECKLACE
ISOBELLE BUNTING
This necklace is made with the triple spiral staircase technique. Gold is the perfect complement for royal blue and rich purple as both colours tend towards the warm section of the colour wheel. This necklace is sophisticated yet it also has a simplicity that is very appealing.

Woodland berries

WOODLAND BERRIES ARE SO ENTICING WITH THEIR GLOSSY RICH REDS AND PURPLES.

The reds and purples of berries look wonderful set against bronze and black and are easily accessorized with silver. These colours can be contrasted with almost any shade of green from lime to jade, including tints and shades. This theme provokes textural interest as well as colour.

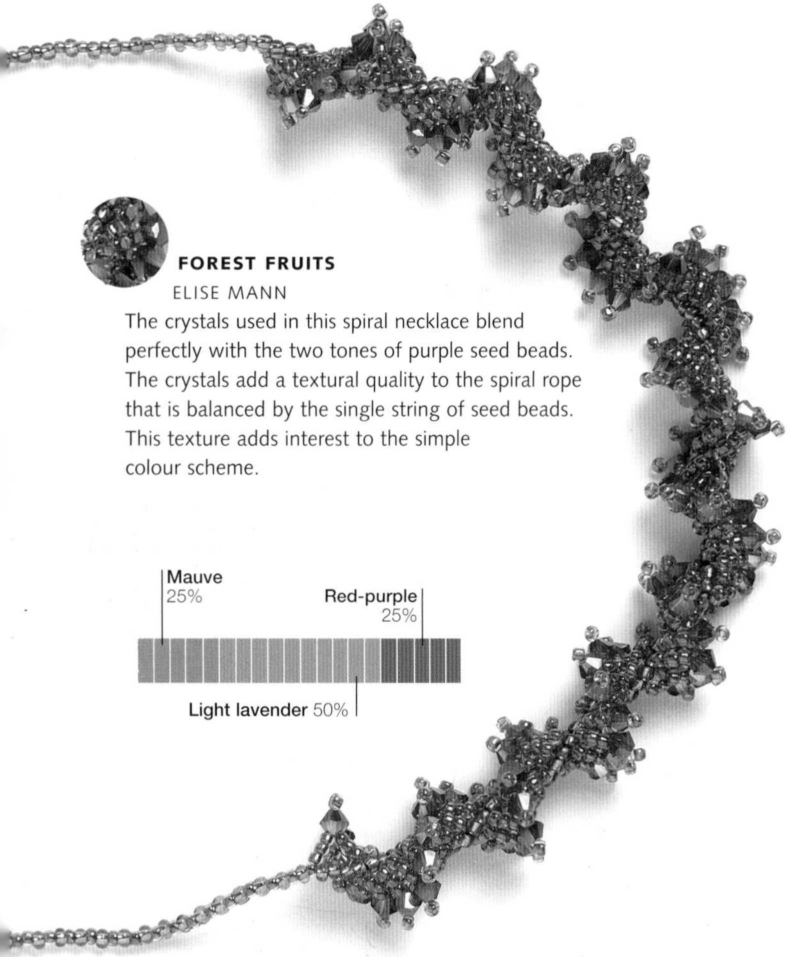

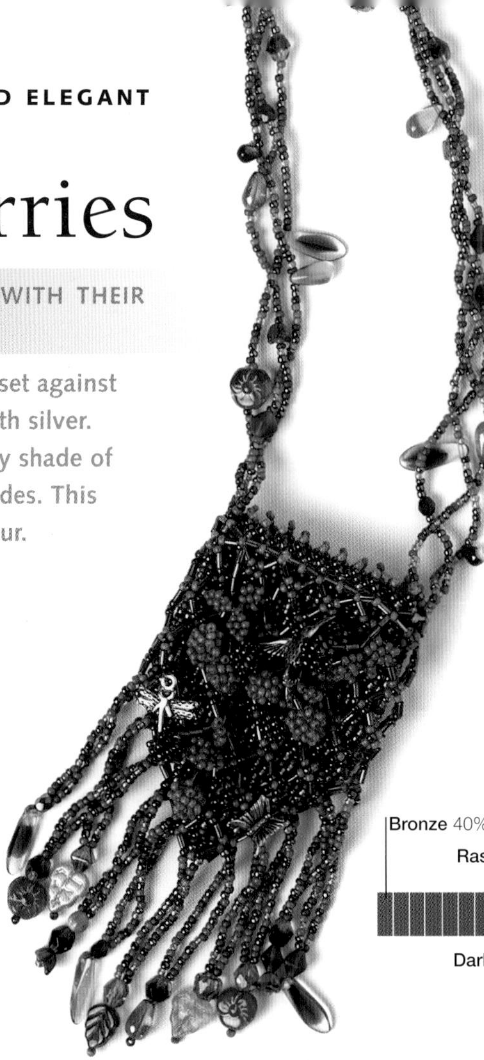

FOREST FRUITS
ELISE MANN

The crystals used in this spiral necklace blend perfectly with the two tones of purple seed beads. The crystals add a textural quality to the spiral rope that is balanced by the single string of seed beads. This texture adds interest to the simple colour scheme.

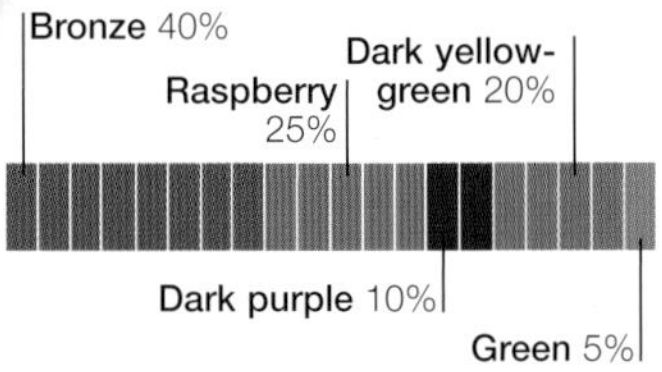

Mauve 25%
Red-purple 25%
Light lavender 50%

Bronze 40%
Raspberry 25%
Dark yellow-green 20%
Dark purple 10%
Green 5%

BLACKBERRIES AND RASPBERRIES
LYNNE WILLIAMS

A bronze background is overlaid with a trellis of bugle beads, reminiscent of the rambling brambles in hedgerows. This is echoed on the twisted necklace strap of the purse. Czech glass leaves and seed bead berries are dotted all over the purse.

Black
30%

Silver
15%

Pale pink
5%

Purple 10%

Raspberry 10%

Navy 20%

Lavender 10%

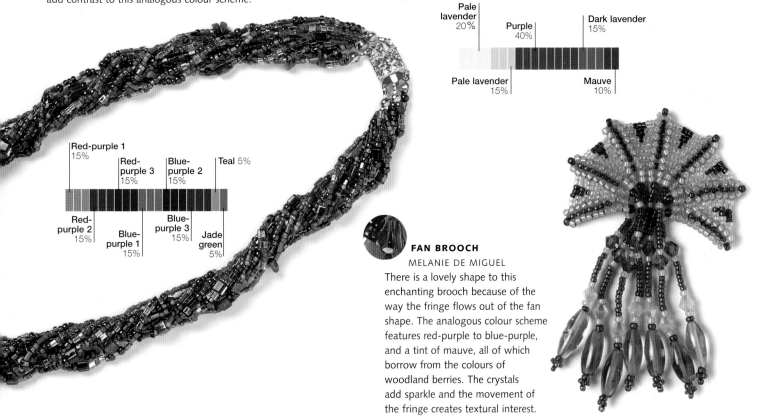

BLACKBERRY FROST
SANDRA WALLACE

Sculptural peyote stitch has been used to create this unusual freeform cuff in an analogous colour scheme of pink, raspberry and purple set against black. The pink is just bright enough to stand out against the darker colours without being too bold. Patches of silver beads glint in the bracelet and the freeform wire shapes add textural interest.

TWISTED STRANDS
GILL HOOPER

This is a beautiful multi-stranded necklace made of red-purple, blue-purple and jade green beads. The twisted strands are strung with a bead mix of mostly seed beads with some larger beads and malachite chips producing a textural quality. The green beads add contrast to this analogous colour scheme.

Pale
lavender
20%

Purple
40%

Dark lavender
15%

Pale lavender
15%

Mauve
10%

Red-purple 1
15%

Red-purple 3
15%

Blue-purple 2
15%

Teal 5%

Red-purple 2
15%

Blue-purple 1
15%

Blue-purple 3
15%

Jade green
5%

FAN BROOCH
MELANIE DE MIGUEL

There is a lovely shape to this enchanting brooch because of the way the fringe flows out of the fan shape. The analogous colour scheme features red-purple to blue-purple, and a tint of mauve, all of which borrow from the colours of woodland berries. The crystals add sparkle and the movement of the fringe creates textural interest.

chapter three
THE PROJECTS

In this chapter ten projects utilizing the colour schemes described in the colour theory chapter are explained step-by-step with a photograph of each finished piece. The projects techniques vary in difficulty from simple stringing to complex stitching. The projects include earrings, a brooch, bracelets and a variety of necklaces. Each project also features four suggestions for alternative colour schemes, so there is guaranteed to be a scheme that will inspire you.

Project 1: Monochromatic earrings

SUBTLE SHADES OF PURPLE COMBINE HARMONIOUSLY IN THESE MONOCHROMATIC EARRINGS.

This geometric design is in a monochromatic colour scheme with shades of purple, from violet to dark plum. The tones of purple change gradually from dark to light, leading the eye.

BEAD STORE

2g plum delica beads

2g purple delica beads

2g violet delica beads

Pair of earring findings

Beading needle and thread

2cm (⁸⁄₁₀ in) wide
4cm (1½ in) high

1 Using approximately 1m (3 feet) of thread and one colour of bead, start at the centre row of the diamond and make an 11-bead ladder.

2 Make rows using brick stitch, decreasing each row by one to form one half of the first diamond.

3 Take the needle back to the centre row and repeat step 2 to form the other half of the diamond.

4 Repeat these steps using the other two bead colours to complete two further diamonds.

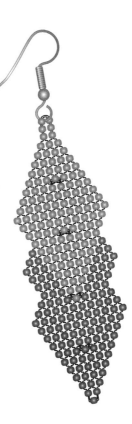

5 To join the diamonds together, place one on top of the other (see diagram).

6 With the thread emerging from a bead on the top diamond, take the needle between the beads through to the bottom diamond. Go through one or two beads, then come back between the beads and through one or two beads on the top diamond.

7 Continue with this until the two diamonds are securely attached.

8 Repeat until all three diamonds have been sewn together. Finish off with a loop of four beads and an earring hook at the top.

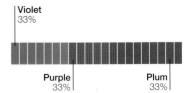

Violet 33%

Purple 33%

Plum 33%

BLUE-GREEN

Cool blue-green is a very versatile colour for a pair of earrings to match a wide range of colours. Paler tones are used here evoking memories of the sea.

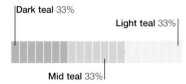

Dark teal 33%

Light teal 33%

Mid teal 33%

CITRUS LEMON AND LIME GREEN

Citrus lemon and pale lime green give a fresh look to these earrings. These colours are reminiscent of early spring days.

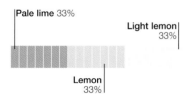

Pale lime 33%

Light lemon 33%

Lemon 33%

PINK AND MAUVE

This feminine colour scheme combines lower intensity tones of pink and mauve. It has a beauty that reminds us of faded roses.

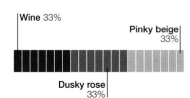

Wine 33%

Pinky beige 33%

Dusky rose 33%

BURNT ORANGE AND BROWN

This warm colour scheme is inspired by the rich colours of autumn. Burnt orange and brown offer a warm but not vivid colour scheme.

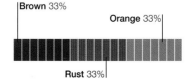

Brown 33%

Orange 33%

Rust 33%

Project 2: Analogous brooch

AN ANALOGOUS COLOUR SCHEME INSPIRED BY ABALONE CREATES A MELLOW EFFECT IN THIS FREEFORM BROOCH.

This brooch was inspired by the colours and patterns found in abalone shell, which change according to the light and evoke the feeling of the sea. Select colours and harmonizing tones from those found in the shell.

BEAD STORE

 Piece of abalone shell

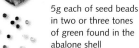 5g each of seed beads in two or three tones of green found in the abalone shell

 3g delica beads in four or more colours toning with the abalone

 Small quantities of feature beads such as pearls, small crystals and green gemstones such as malachite and peridot

Small piece of thick interfacing

Small piece of leather

Brooch back

Strong glue

Beading needle and thread

3.8cm (2½ in) in diameter

1 Abalone shells are often domed, so glue a circle of interfacing to the back of the disc, leaving a border of abalone.

2 At this stage, if you are using a bar-type brooch back rather than the circle suggested, stitch the bar to a piece of leather (preferably in a toning colour), cut into a circle slightly larger than the abalone disc, then glue it to the back of the abalone. (If the circular brooch back is to be used, this will be attached at the end.)

3 Back stitch a circle of seed beads in a variety of greens closely around the perimeter of the abalone disc.

4 Stitch rows of peyote in the seed beads up around the edge of the disc, beading into the original stitched row, with one row beaded tightly over the surface of the disc, so that the edge is hidden.

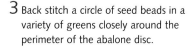

5 Stitch petals in freeform peyote, starting from the back edge of the disc, using seed beads for the first three or so rows, which will hardly show, then using delica beads which give a more delicate effect. By increasing the number of beads in each row (which can be done by adding two beads and one bead alternately between the beads of the previous row, or by inserting semi-precious stone chips or larger beads) and by adding textured beads such as crystals, pearls and tiny gemstones, a wavy effect is achieved. (The textured feature beads will be shown off to best effect if they are near the top of the petal.) Vary the colours in each petal, but use several of the same colour bead in each row to give a linear rather than a spotty design.

6 Once the first row of petals has been formed at the back, gradually work forwards so that the front petals curl over the surface of the abalone. Pearls and gemstones can be stitched into the folds of the petals.

7 Once the petals form a harmonious shape round the disc and the brooch is the desired size, glue the circular brooch back into position.

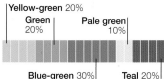

Yellow-green 20%
Green 20%
Pale green 10%
Blue-green 30%
Teal 20%

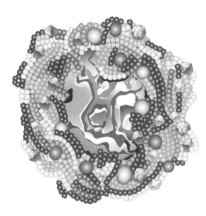

RED-PURPLE AND RED-ORANGE
Cream unites the colours of red-purple and red-orange, which otherwise might not be desirable together. This unusual colour scheme is inspired by the colour of sunset.

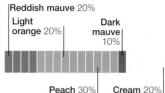

Reddish mauve 20%
Light orange 20%
Dark mauve 10%
Peach 30%
Cream 20%

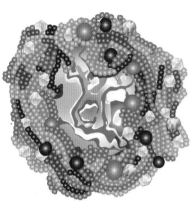

RED, ORANGE AND YELLOW
Darker shades of red, orange and yellow merge to form this rich colour scheme. The differences in tonal value add variety to this scheme.

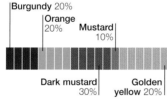

Burgundy 20%
Orange 20%
Mustard 10%
Dark mustard 30%
Golden yellow 20%

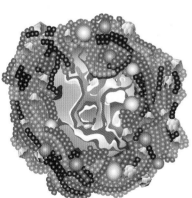

PURPLE AND BLUE
An amethyst cabochon would be the ideal replacement for the abalone for this blue and purple colour scheme. The blue tones add interest to this scheme.

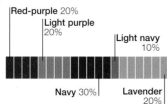

Red-purple 20%
Light purple 20%
Light navy 10%
Navy 30%
Lavender 20%

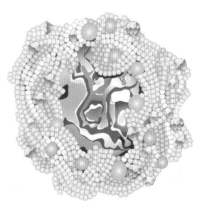

RED AND YELLOW PASTELS
Pale clear colours of spring are used in this pastel colour scheme. Warm tints of red and yellow are blended together for a delicate colour scheme.

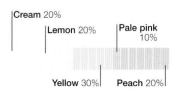

Cream 20%
Lemon 20%
Pale pink 10%
Yellow 30%
Peach 20%

Project 3: Complementary colours

MIX COMPLEMENTARY COLOURS TO BRING
VIBRANCY TO THIS PRETTY STRUNG NECKLACE.

This stunning fuchsia and lime necklace is very contemporary.
The 'oily jade' and crystals add flair to a simple, strung design,
which makes it look more glamourous.

BEAD STORE

26 x 8mm faceted
Serpentine (oily jade)
beads (A)

18mm carved oval
Serpentine beads (B)

2 x 30mm large oval
Serpentine beads (C)

18 x 8mm fuchsia
round faceted
Swarovski crystals (D)

20 x 6mm fuchsia
bicone Swarovski
crystals (E)

Silver clasp

1.2cm (½ in) silver gimp
(bullion), optional

Beading needle and thread

45cm (18 in)
long

1 Thread the needle with about
1.5m (60 in) of thread and use
the thread double.

2 Thread on the following
sequence of beads:
Left-side section: E, A,
E, A, E, A, D, A, E, A,
D, B, D, A, E, C.
Centre section,
upper: E, A, E, A, D,
B, D, A, D, B, D, A,
D, B, D, A, E, A, E.
Right-side section:
C, E, A, D, B, D, A,
E, A, D, A, E, A, E,
A, E.

3 Thread the needle with
another thread about
1.5m (60 in) long and
use double.

4 Take the thread through the entire
left-side section, then thread on
the following sequence of beads:
Centre section, lower: E, A, E, A,
D, B, D, A, E, A, D, B, D, A, E, A,
D, B, D, A, E, A, E.

5 Take the thread through the entire right-
side section to complete the necklace.

6 Attach one side of the clasp to
the left side of the necklace by
going through a 0.6cm (¼ in)
piece of gimp (optional), then
the clasp. All four threads will
go through the gimp, but you
will find it easier to thread
one or two at a time.

7 Pass the needle back
through two beads,
knot before the next
bead, go through
another bead, and pull
the knot into the bead.
Do this three or four
more times. Cut the
thread close to the bead
after threading through
another bead.

8 Repeat steps 6 and 7 on the right side of
the necklace, making sure all the threads
are pulled taut before attaching the clasp.

Oily jade 60%

Fuchsia crystals
40%

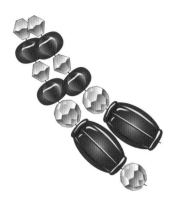

BLUE AND ORANGE
Blue and orange are reminiscent of the Mediterranean. The high intensity orange is used in the smaller proportion here to balance the advancing effect of this warm colour.

Blue 60%

Orange 40%

PASTEL PEACH AND BLUE
These pastel tones are inspired by the Arizona landscape. The peach-coloured rocks set against a blue summer sky are emulated here.

Pastel blue 60%

Peach 40%

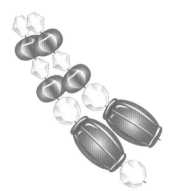

PURPLE AND YELLOW TINTS
Tints of purple and yellow are the colours used for this delicate colour scheme. Pastel tones harmonize very well as they are less intense.

Lavender 60%

Pale lemon 40%

GREEN AND RED
Green leaves with red berries are the inspiration for this complementary scheme. These two colours fight for attention if used in equal proportions so the warmer red is given the greater proportion.

Red 60%

Green 40%

Project 4: Woven bracelet

USE A SUBTLE SPLIT COMPLEMENTARY SCHEME TO
MAKE THIS DELICATE LOOM-WOVEN BRACELET.

This loom-woven bracelet is worked in a split complementary colour scheme of yellow-orange combined with subtly different shades and finishes of blue and purple.

BEAD STORE

5g gold-lined transparent blue size 8 seed beads

5g yellow-orange delica beads

5g blue delica beads

5g opaque matt purple delica beads

5g transparent purple delica beads

Two large transparent yellow-orange beads

Beading needle and thread

Bead loom

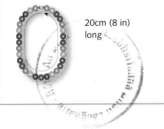
20cm (8 in) long

1 The bracelet will be 11 beads deep so warp your loom with 12 warp threads. These should be at least 50cm (20 in) long so that you will be able to make the bracelet fastenings from remaining warp threads when finishing off.

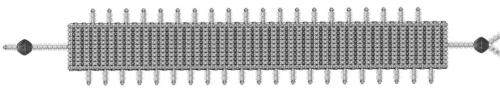

2 Weave the first four rows following the sequence shown in the illustration above.

3 When you weave the fifth row thread on two seed beads and a yellow-orange delica bead to make the first tassel. Take the needle and thread through and around the delica bead, back through the seed beads, and finish weaving the row as usual so that the first tassel sits on the right-hand side of the piece. Pull taut.

4 Weave the next row.

5 When you weave row seven, add the tassel to the beginning of the row before weaving (instead of the end) so that it sits on the left-hand side of the piece. Weave the remainder of the pattern to the end. Add tassels where appropriate.

6 When your design is long enough, remove it from the loom. Carefully weave all except the two centre warp threads on each end of the bracelet back into the piece.

7 On one end of the bracelet thread seven blue seed beads, a large yellow-orange bead, two further blue seed beads, and then a yellow-orange delica bead onto the two remaining warps, take both threads back through the beads, and weave them back into the bracelet securely.

8 At the other end of the bracelet thread five blue seed beads, one large amber bead, and 17 further blue seed beads onto the two remaining warp threads, but this time make a beaded loop of the 17 seed beads, then take the thread back through the other beads. Weave the remaining warp threads back into the bracelet securely.

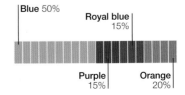

Blue 50% | Royal blue 15%
Purple 15% | Orange 20%

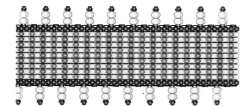

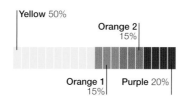

YELLOW, ORANGE AND PURPLE

The sunny yellow and orange in this bracelet are enhanced by the small proportion of purple. Warm colours with their complement can be glorious.

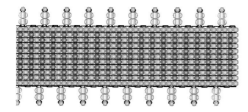

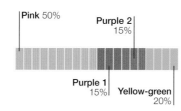

PINK, PURPLE AND YELLOW-GREEN

Yellow-green adds a sparkle to this scheme which uses tints of red and purple. These colours are seen in abundance in a garden in bloom.

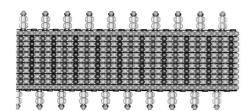

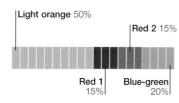

ORANGE, RED AND BLUE-GREEN

Orange and red can be quite a daring combination of colours. The bright blue-green adds a contrast that unites the whole colour scheme.

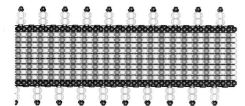

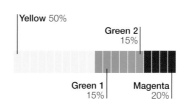

YELLOW, GREEN AND MAGENTA

The bright yellow and green used here is given an added boost with the small proportion of magenta. This is an energetic and vivid colour scheme.

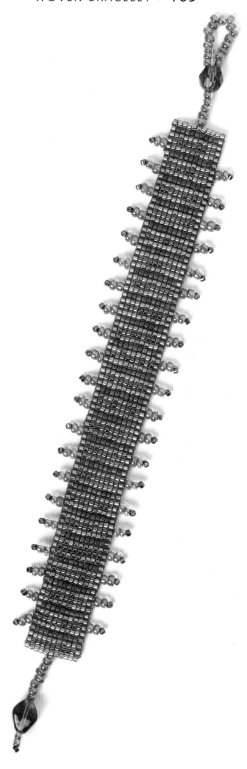

Project 5: Triadic spiral bracelet

THE TRIADIC COLOUR SCHEME IN THIS BRACELET CREATES A STRIKING BUT BALANCED EFFECT.

This design is based on a triadic colour scheme of red, blue, and yellow. White has been added to the red and blue to give pink and pastel blue, whilst grey has been added to yellow to make khaki.

BEAD STORE

 11g pastel blue size 5 triangle beads (A)

 3g pastel blue size 11 seed beads (B)

 7g 4mm khaki crystal bicones (C)

 1g khaki delica beads (D)

 3g pink size 11 hex beads (E)

 3g pink size 11 seed beads (F)

Clasp

Beading needle and thread

 20cm (8 in) long

1 Use as long a piece of thread as possible and pick up the beads in the following order: one A, three B, one C, two D, one E and four F.

2 Leave a long tail and then tie the thread into a loop.

3 Take the needle back through the attached A.

4 Thread on one A and three B then take the needle through the attached C.

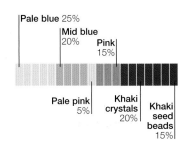

5 Thread on one C and two D then take the needle through the attached E.

6 Thread on one E and four F then take the needle back through the A just added. Repeat this sequence from step 4 until the bracelet is the desired length.

7 For the final round, miss out the axis beads (A, C and E) and use the filler beads only (B, D and F).

8 Add a clasp to either end of the bracelet and sew in all the loose ends.

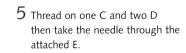

Pale blue 25%
Mid blue 20%
Pink 15%
Pale pink 5%
Khaki crystals 20%
Khaki seed beads 15%

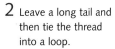

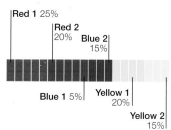

RED, YELLOW AND BLUE

Primary colours are casual and fun. The primaries are used here with a greater proportion of red and yellow, giving a warm colour scheme with blue used as a contrast.

Red 1 25%
Red 2 20%
Blue 2 15%
Blue 1 5%
Yellow 1 20%
Yellow 2 15%

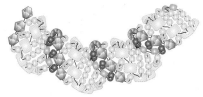

LIME GREEN, PEACH AND BLUE-VIOLET

Lime green, peach and blue-violet is quite a bright colour scheme. It would be good to choose beads with a variety of finishes to unify the scheme.

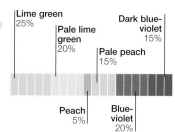

Lime green 25%
Pale lime green 20%
Dark blue-violet 15%
Pale peach 15%
Peach 5%
Blue-violet 20%

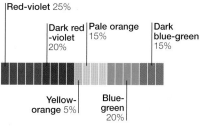

RED-VIOLET, YELLOW-ORANGE AND BLUE-GREEN

Red-violet, yellow-orange and blue-green together are reminiscent of the colours used in Indian silks. Used in these proportions this bracelet would be bold and well-balanced.

Red-violet 25%
Dark red-violet 20%
Pale orange 15%
Dark blue-green 15%
Yellow-orange 5%
Blue-green 20%

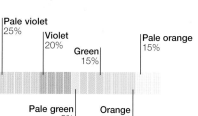

PASTEL VIOLET, GREEN AND ORANGE

Pastels are used for this scheme. Toning down colours with white makes them much less vivid, giving a totally different appearance.

Pale violet 25%
Violet 20%
Green 15%
Pale orange 15%
Pale green 5%
Orange 20%

Project 6: Tetradic necklace

THIS VIBRANT NECKLACE OFFERS A GREAT
DEAL OF VARIETY AND CONTRAST.

The simplicity of the rope and the bands of teal give uniformity to the
design, whilst the tetradic colour scheme provides the striking contrast.

BEAD STORE

7g teal size 11 seed beads

1g each of size 11 seed
beads in the following
colours: pale teal, lime,
green, raspberry and coral
(several shades of coral were
used for variety)

1g each of raspberry and
dark coral size 5 triangles

1g each of size 8 seed beads
in teal, lime and coral

1g green size 7 seed beads

1g each of raspberry and
lime size 6 seed beads

1g raspberry size 10
triangles

1g 3mm teal squares

1g each 4mm coral and
raspberry squares

Beading needle and thread

50cm (20 in)
long

1 Stitch a ladder of six teal size 11 seed beads.
Join the first and the last bead to form a ring
and exit at the top of the first bead.

2 Work tubular herringbone stitch in
teal size 11 seed beads as follows.
Pick up two beads, go down the
second bead and up the third
bead, pick up two beads, go
down the fourth bead and up
the fifth bead, pick up two
beads and go down the sixth
bead. Go up the first bead in
the initial row and also the
first bead in the second row.
You are now ready to start the
third row.

3 Continue working the tubular
herringbone stitch as in step
2 for the remainder of the
necklace, changing colours and
sizes as follows.

4 Always working in size 11 seed beads
work ten rows of teal including the
ladder stitch row, then one row of coral,
nine rows of teal, one row of raspberry,
and nine rows of teal.

5 First contrast section: work one row lime size
11, one row coral size 11, one row raspberry
size 10 triangles, one row teal size 8, one
row coral size 8, one row raspberry size 6.
Work one row coral size 8, one row teal size
8, one row raspberry size 10 triangles,
one row coral size 11, one row lime
size 11.

6 Work nine rows of teal in
size 11 beads between each
coloured section.

7 Second contrast section:
work one row each of
raspberry, pale teal and lime
size 11, work one row each
of teal and pale coral size
8, work one row green size
7 and one row coral 4-mm
squares. Work one row
green size 7, one row each
of pale coral and teal size 8,
one row each of lime, pale
teal and raspberry size 11.

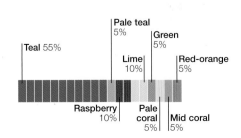

8 Third contrast section: work one row each of pale coral and green size 11, one row raspberry size 10 triangles, one row mid-coral size 8, one row teal 3-mm squares, one row raspberry size 5 triangles. Work one row teal 3-mm squares, one row mid-coral size 8, one row raspberry size 10 triangles, one row each of green and pale coral size 11.

9 Fourth contrast section: work one row each of lime, raspberry and teal size 11, one row each of pale coral, teal and lime size 8, one row dark coral size 5 triangles, one row lime size 6, one row dark coral size 6, one row each of lime, teal and pale coral in size 8, one row each of teal, raspberry and lime in size 11.

10 Fifth contrast section: work one row each of raspberry and pale coral size 11, one row each of teal, lime and coral size 8, one row green size 7, one row raspberry size 6, one row teal 3-mm squares, one row dark coral size 5 triangles, one row teal 3-mm squares, one row raspberry size 6, one row green size 7, one row each of coral, lime, and teal size 8, one row each of pale coral and raspberry size 11.

11 Repeat fourth, third, second and first contrast sections for the necklace to be symmetrical.

12 Finish the necklace by working nine rows of teal, then one row of raspberry, nine rows of teal, one row of coral and ten rows of teal. Work up and down the beads in the last row to join the beads together and finish off.

13 Attach a clasp by going through a size 6 bead, then the clasp, back through the size 6 bead, and into the beadwork. Repeat three times, then fasten off the thread in the beadwork, knotting between the beads.

continued
on page 114

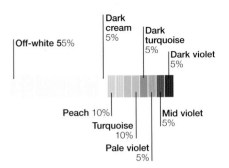

PEACH, TURQUOISE, VIOLET AND OFF-WHITE

Peach, turquoise and violet are set against an off-white background. These lovely soft and gentle colours would be elegant worn against a pale background.

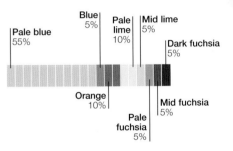

PALE BLUE, ORANGE, LIME AND FUCHSIA

This is a pretty summer colour scheme with pale blue as the predominant colour. Accents of orange, lime and fuchsia add vitality to the calm blue.

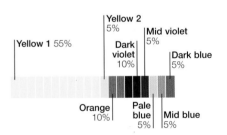

YELLOW, VIOLET, BLUE AND ACCENTS OF ORANGE

This necklace is not for the fainthearted! Bright sunny yellow is contrasted with violet and blue for this stunning scheme. Accents of orange complete the necklace.

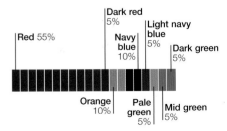

BRIGHT RED, BLUES AND GREENS

This bold colour scheme would make a stunning necklace for winter. Bright red is toned down with the addition of darker blues and greens.

Project 7: Warm-toned choker

THE WARM COLOUR SCHEME USED IN THIS CHOKER CREATES A VIVID AND BOLD PIECE OF JEWELLERY.

This choker is based on three-bead square netting stitch embellished with a warm palette of garnets, corals, and pearls. The texture is given by the diversity of the beads that have been incorporated into the design.

BEAD STORE

For the right-angle weave base:
7g each of size 11 gold and garnet seed beads and 5g coral size 11 seed beads

For the embellishment:
String of drilled garnets

String of coral-coloured beads

7g each of a variety of garnet-coloured beads such as cubes, size 6 beads, teardrops and crystals

5g each of coral-coloured beads such as size 5 triangles and fire-polished crystals

Choker fastening finding

Beading needle and thread

30cm (12 in) long, excluding the clasp

1 This design is 30cm (12 in) long excluding the clasp, and each square is 6mm (¼ in) square. The design can be lengthened or shortened as required by adding or subtracting rows of squares in the centre or at each end, but should end with two squares. Note that the gold beads are only used for the outside edges of the choker and as dividing lines between the garnet and coral sections if desired. Where the right-angle weave base is referred to, work only in size 11 seed beads in coral, garnet or gold.

2 Make the square netting base with size 11 seed beads following the colour chart in Diagram 1. Thread six gold and six coral seed beads, leaving an end 10cm (4 in) long, then go through the beads again and pull up into a loop (see Diagram 2, on page 116).

3 Knot the two threads together to secure the loop, thread a needle onto the short end, pull it through three beads and cut off the thread. Make square 2 using the long thread by passing the needle through six gold beads and three coral beads. Then add three coral

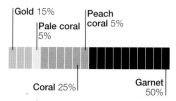

beads and six gold beads, joining them into a square by going back down through three coral beads of the original square (see Diagram 3, on page 116).

4 To make square 3 go through the three coral beads at the base of the second square then pick up nine coral beads. Go back through the three coral beads at the base of the second square and three coral beads at the side of this square.

5 To make square 4 add three garnet-coloured beads and six gold beads. Pass through nine beads of square 3 – these are the three coral beads at the side, the three beads at the base, and the three beads on the other side. Then pass through the three coral beads at the base of square 1.

Gold 15%　Peach coral 5%
Pale coral 5%
Coral 25%　Garnet 50%

continued on page 116

6 To make square 5, thread on six coral beads and go back through three coral beads at the side of square 3, three coral beads at the base of square 1, then three coral beads at the side of square 5.

7 To make square 6, thread on three coral and six gold beads and join these up to square 5 as shown, pass down through the three beads of the fifth square and three beads at the base of the sixth square. Carry on with the net following Diagram 1 for colours until the desired length has been reached.

8 Attach the clasp firmly by adding three seed beads either side of the clasp holes to make loops, go through these several times, and strengthen the fastening by going around the netting again between threading through the loops. Go through more beads of the netting at the end and knot the end of the thread before going through more beads and cutting off the end of the thread.

9 Knot in another thread at one end of the choker and begin to fill in the net using diagonal lines of the same beads as shown. Start from the corner of the net as shown in Diagram 4, thread on the beads and go diagonally across the net and thread the needle back through the net to attach the new beads. Repeat the process so that two threads go through the embellishing beads, then carry on to the next square and repeat the process in the next square.

10 Keep the pattern correct so that initially you have a diagonal row of coral fire-polished crystals, then a row of coral triangles, then a row of coral pearls. The next three diagonal rows would use garnet-coloured beads. It doesn't really matter which embellishing beads are used as long as the diagonal lines are correct and the garnet-coloured beads embellish the garnet squares and coral-coloured beads embellish the coral squares.

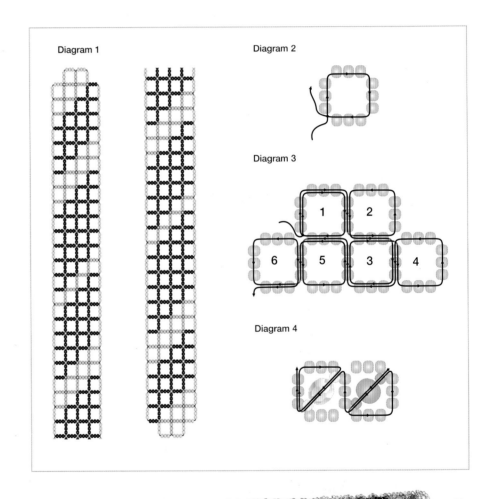

Diagram 1

Diagram 2

Diagram 3

Diagram 4

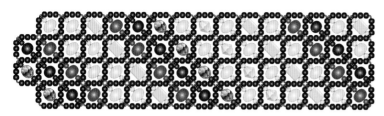

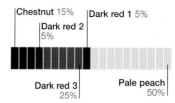

Chestnut 15% Dark red 1 5%
Dark red 2 5%
Dark red 3 25%
Pale peach 50%

DARK RED, CHESTNUT AND PALE PEACH

These rich, warm browns and reds are reminiscent of the shiny coats of horse chestnuts. Pale peach is used as a contrast with dark brown accents.

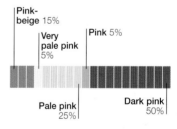

Pale cream 15%
Pale yellow 5%
Ochre 5%
Yellow 25%
Dark ochre 50%

OCHRE, PALE YELLOW AND CREAM

Warm colours need not be vivid, as demonstrated by the yellow tones used here. These are the ochre hues of dried grasses, which are brightened with the addition of pale yellow and cream.

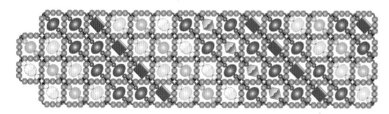

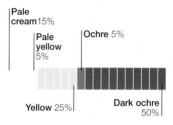

Pink-beige 15%
Very pale pink 5%
Pink 5%
Pale pink 25%
Dark pink 50%

ROSE PINK AND BEIGE

The warm rose pinks in this colour scheme are quite delicate. Adding beige makes the colour scheme more interesting.

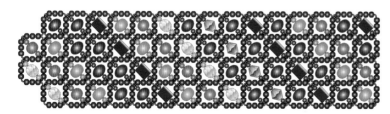

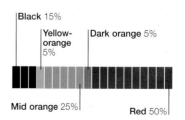

Black 15%
Yellow-orange 5%
Dark orange 5%
Mid orange 25%
Red 50%

RED, ORANGE AND BLACK

Red and orange, the warmest colours, are stunning set against a black background. This colour scheme is inspired by the hot lava of a volcano.

Project 8: Cool-toned lariat

**THE COOL BLUE PALETTE NEVER FAILS
TO BRING A FEELING OF TRANQUILLITY.**

The calmness created by the blue colouring is echoed by the simplicity
of this design, with just enough interest created by adding crystals and
larger beads.

BEAD STORE

 20g cobalt transparent
AB size 8 beads (A)

 20g white-lined aqua
size 8 hex beads (B)

 15g transparent aqua
size 11 seed beads (C)

 38 x 4mm aquamarine
Swarovski crystal
bicones

 7 x 6mm aqua round
cat's eye beads and
4 x 8mm aqua oval
cat's eye beads

1 x 22mm blue/aqua
lampwork bead

Beading needle and thread

 106cm (42 in)
long including
fringes

1 Using at least 2m (6 feet) of
nymo beading thread,
pick up beads in the
following order: four
A, two C, one B and
two C. Tie the beads
into a circle. Pass back
through the four A
beads (see Diagram 1).

2 Pick up beads in the
following order: one
A, two C, one B and
two C. Push the beads
down onto the work (see
Diagram 2). Pass the needle
back through the last three
A beads in the rope and the
A just added (see Diagram
3). Pull the thread taut.

3 Position the beads just added next
to the previous outside beads.

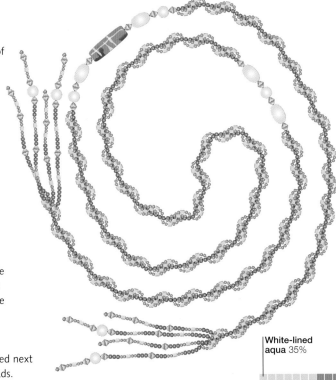

White-lined
aqua 35%

Cobalt
25%

Transparent aqua
40%

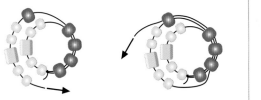

Diagram 1   Diagram 2   Diagram 3

4 Repeat steps 2 to 3 until the rope is 23cm (9 in) long.

5 Thread on a crystal, a round cat's eye, a crystal, an oval cat's eye, a crystal, a lampwork bead, a crystal, an oval cat's eye, a crystal, a round cat's eye and finally a crystal.

6 Pick up beads in the following order: four A, two C, one B, and two C. Pass back through the four A beads. Repeat steps 2 through 3 twice, then pass back through the core and the strung beads into the first section, turn and pass back through the beads again to get to the second section. This strengthens the strung section.

7 Carry on with the second section of rope until this section measures 38cm (15 in).

8 Thread on a crystal, an oval cat's eye, a crystal, a round cat's eye, a crystal, an oval cat's eye and a crystal.

9 Repeat step 6, then carry on beading until this third section is 20cm (8 in) long.

10 Thread on about 5cm (2 in) of beads, using seed beads, crystals and cat's eyes, ending with a size 11 seed bead. Pass back through all the beads except the bottom seed bead. Stitch into the core and down the outside beads (which were added last). Make another fringe. Repeat the fringes on another two sections of outside beads.

11 Complete the other end of the lariat to match.

continued on page 120

PALE, MEDIUM AND DARK GREEN

Green is a restful colour, this is not surprising as there is an abundance of it in nature. Leafy tones of pale, mid and dark green are combined here.

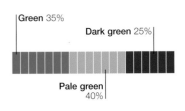

Green 35%

Dark green 25%

Pale green 40%

TURQUOISE AND DARK BLUE-GREEN

These lovely blue-greens are evocative of the sea on a bright day, from the turquoise of the shallows to the darker blue-green of deeper waters.

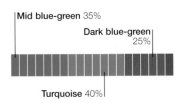

Mid blue-green 35%

Dark blue-green 25%

Turquoise 40%

LAVENDER AND DARK PURPLE

Lavender is said to be calming and the colour reflects this. Tones from light lavender to dark blue-purple are used in this cool colour scheme.

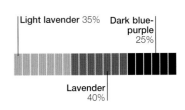

Light lavender 35%

Dark blue-purple 25%

Lavender 40%

PALE GREEN, PALE BLUE AND CLEAR CRYSTAL

Very pale green and blue are combined with clear crystal beads in this cool colour scheme. The cool schemes would not be complete without one inspired by snow and ice.

Crystal white 35%

Icy pale blue 25%

Icy pale green 40%

Project 9: Neutral necklace

NEUTRAL COLOUR SCHEMES ARE SO VERSATILE THAT THIS NECKLACE WOULD GO WELL WITH ANY OUTFIT.

Creamy tones, especially when combined with gold, give the feeling of opulence, creating a classic understated look. This off-white and beige colour scheme could be worn with most other colours.

BEAD STORE

 28 x 5mm mother-of-pearl beads (A), 12 x 10mm mother-of-pearl beads (B), and 6 x 10mm disc beads (C)

 5g topaz gold lustre size 8 beads (T)

 7g cream matt size 6 beads and 35 beige matt size 6 beads

 100 cream pearl size 8 beads

 100 cream matt size 11 beads and 100 beige matt size 11 beads

 200 cream lustre delica beads

Beading needle and thread

Gold clasp

5 pieces of drinking straw or plastic tubing about 5cm (2 in) long

 45cm (18 in) long

1 Stitch a ladder of beads, three beads high and seven beads wide, using the cream matt and beige matt size 6 beads and just over 1m (3 feet) of thread, pick up one cream, one beige, two cream, one beige and one cream bead. Push the beads down to the middle of the thread so that there is 0.5m (18 in) left. This is used to work the other half of the bead.

2 Pass back through the first three beads (cream, beige and cream), then down through the second three beads (cream, beige and cream). Add three more beads (cream, beige and cream), and go down through the last stack of three beads, and up through the beads just added. Continue in this way until there are seven stacks of beads in total.

continued on page 122

3 Pass back through all the stacks to strengthen and align the beads. Join the first and last stack together to form a ring. Insert the straw or tubing into the ring.

4 Pick up two cream pearl size 8 beads and work brick stitch into the first space on the ladder. Work another eight seed beads into the top of the ladder (ten beads in total). You will need to ensure that the seed beads are evenly spaced around the bead. Join the first and last bead together.

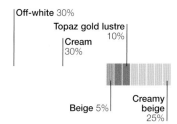

Off-white 30%
Topaz gold lustre 10%
Cream 30%
Beige 5%
Creamy beige 25%

5 Next row, work one topaz gold lustre size 8 bead into each space on the previous row (ten beads in total).

6 Work the next three rows as follows: cream matt size 11, beige matt size 11, cream lustre delica beads. There will be ten beads in each row. The decreasing size of the beads shapes the beaded bead.

7 Work this final row to neaten the edge so that no thread shows. Pick up a delica bead, pass down through the next bead on the previous row, and then up through the adjacent bead. Pick up another bead and repeat the sequence, continuing in this way until there are five beads in this row and you are back to the beginning. Pick up another bead and work in the reverse direction filling in the five spaces. Thread through all the beads in the ring twice. Finish off the thread.

8 Using the 0.5m (18 in) of thread left at the beginning, follow steps 4 through to 7 to work the other half of the bead to match.

9 Make four more beads in this way.

To make the necklace:

1 String beads in the following order: one T, one A, one T, one A, one T, one A, one T (one B, one C, one B, one T, one A, one T, one A, the beaded bead, one A, one T, one A, one T). Repeat the sequence in brackets four more times then add one B, one C, one B, one T, one A, one T, one A, one T, one A and one T.

2 Attach a clasp at each end of the necklace.

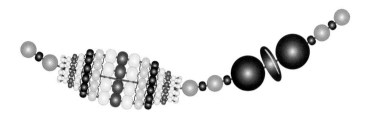

METALLIC GREYS
These greys reflect the colours of cold metals, from the pale grey of silver to the darker grey of steel. Haematite and jet would also blend very well with this colour scheme.

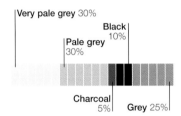

Very pale grey 30%
Black 10%
Pale grey 30%
Charcoal 5%
Grey 25%

PINK-TINTED PALE GREY AND BEIGE
Pale grey and beige, both with a pink tint, are the foundation for this colour scheme. Dark and medium brown are used as accent colours.

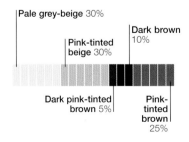

Pale grey-beige 30%
Pink-tinted beige 30%
Dark brown 10%
Dark pink-tinted brown 5%
Pink-tinted brown 25%

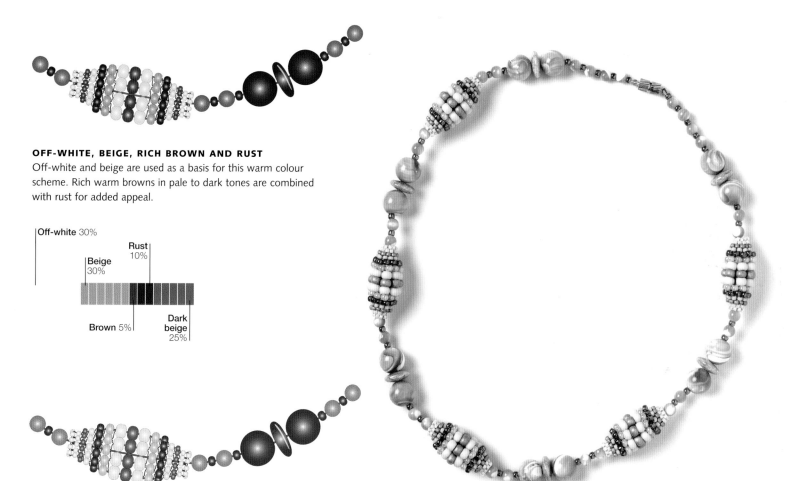

OFF-WHITE, BEIGE, RICH BROWN AND RUST

Off-white and beige are used as a basis for this warm colour scheme. Rich warm browns in pale to dark tones are combined with rust for added appeal.

Off-white 30%

Beige
30%

Rust
10%

Brown 5%

Dark
beige
25%

COOL GREY-BEIGE AND GREY-BROWN

These are the colours of rocks and pebbles along the coast. Cooler tones of grey-beige and grey-brown are combined here. These neutrals combine well with many other colours.

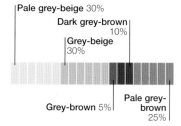

Pale grey-beige 30%

Dark grey-brown
10%

Grey-beige
30%

Grey-brown 5%

Pale grey-
brown
25%

Project 10: Muted necklace

THE MUTED COLOURS IN THE FOCAL BEAD ARE THE INSPIRATION FOR THIS STYLISH NECKLACE.

The earth tones blend well together in this necklace because they are low in intensity, whilst the texture of the beadwork contrasts well with the smooth focal bead.

BEAD STORE

5g slate blue size 11 seed beads

10g very dark moss green size 11 seed beads

8g rust size 11 seed beads

15g of a mix of size 11 seed beads in the following colours: amber, rust, very dark moss green, other muted greens, blue, beige and mauve

8g of a mix of size 8 seed beads in brown, very dark purple, amber, and rust

1g size 15 seed beads in a toning colour

Focal bead

Beading needle and thread

Clasp

48cm (19 in) long

1 Thread on a stop bead plus the number of slate blue size 11 seed beads required to make a 23cm (9 in) length for section A of the necklace. This length will shrink by about 1.5cm (½ in) when completed.

2 Using size 11 seed beads, pick up one rust, one dark moss green and one rust bead and go through the third bead from the end. *Pick up one rust, one dark moss green and one rust size 11 seed bead, miss a bead, pass through the next bead. Repeat from * to end of row. (See Diagram 1.)

3 Go through the last bead then up through the first three beads to the top, ready to start the next row.

4 Pick up five beads from the bead size 11 bead mix and pass through the top bead (the centre one of the three beads). Repeat all along the row. (See Diagram 2.)

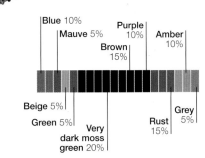

Blue 10%
Mauve 5%
Purple 10%
Brown 15%
Amber 10%
Beige 5%
Green 5%
Very dark moss green 20%
Rust 15%
Grey 5%

5 Repeat steps 2 to 4 on the other side of the central row of blue seed beads. The necklace section will start to spiral, but for clarity the diagrams show it without the spiral.

6 This step gives you a chance to use your own creativity. Work strands of seven to nine beads, including the size 8 beads, passing through one of the five beads added in step 4 and twisting them around the core to another section of five beads. (See Diagram 3.) This step is free-form. These strands work around the necklace adding another layer of embellishment to the netting. This will give a fuller appearance to the necklace.

7 Join a new thread onto one end of this section and thread on the same number of size 15 seed beads as the length of the focal bead. Thread on the focal bead, which should cover all the size 15 beads. This is for protection of the thread as focal beads usually have large holes.

8 Repeat steps 1 through 7 for section B of the necklace.

9 Attach a clasp.

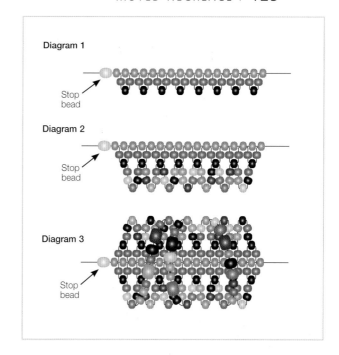

Diagram 1
Stop bead

Diagram 2
Stop bead

Diagram 3
Stop bead

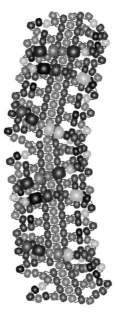

LAVENDER AND ROSE
These soft tones of purple and pink are reminiscent of lavender and roses in an old-fashioned border. This is a very feminine and elegant colour scheme.

Medium pink 10%
Very pale pink 5%
Mauve 10%
Dark violet 15%
Plum 10%
Pale pink 5%
Pale mauve 5%
Grey pink 15%
Dark plum 5%
Dull mauve 20%

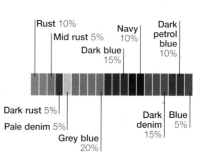

MUTED BLUE AND ORANGE
These complementary tones of blue and orange have been muted to perfection. Tones of denim blue have been given a boost with the rich colours of tanned leather.

Rust 10%
Mid rust 5%
Navy 10%
Dark petrol blue 10%
Dark blue 15%
Dark rust 5%
Pale denim 5%
Grey blue 20%
Dark denim 15%
Blue 5%

continued on page 126

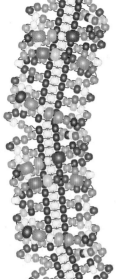

OCHRE AND GREEN

This colour scheme shows the ochres and greens of autumn moorland with its dried vegetation and grasses. Vegetation in autumn is often more muted than in summer sunshine.

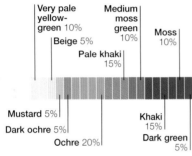

Very pale yellow-green 10%
Beige 5%
Pale khaki 15%
Medium moss green 10%
Moss 10%
Mustard 5%
Dark ochre 5%
Ochre 20%
Khaki 15%
Dark green 5%

BURGUNDY, RUSSET, BEIGE AND BROWN

Here, rich tones of burgundy and russet are set against a background of beige and brown. This combination shows that lower intensity colours need not be dull.

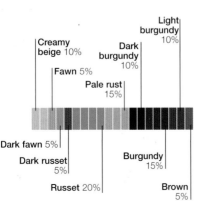

Creamy beige 10%
Fawn 5%
Pale rust 15%
Dark burgundy 10%
Light burgundy 10%
Dark fawn 5%
Dark russet 5%
Russet 20%
Burgundy 15%
Brown 5%

Index

The colour wheel

The colour wheel shows how the primary colours relate to each other, and how mixing two or more colours together creates new colours. A colour wheel is a valuable tool for beaders when devising new colour schemes.

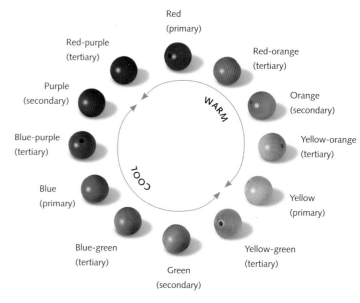

Red (primary)

Red-purple (tertiary)

Red-orange (tertiary)

Purple (secondary)

Orange (secondary)

Blue-purple (tertiary)

Yellow-orange (tertiary)

Blue (primary)

Yellow (primary)

Blue-green (tertiary)

Yellow-green (tertiary)

Green (secondary)

WARM

COOL

TETRADIC COLOUR SCHEMES
Tetradic colour schemes consist of two colours from either side of the colour wheel: two sets of complementary colours.

ANALOGOUS COLOURS
Analogous colours are any three to four colours that are adjacent to each other on the colour wheel, for example, blue, blue-green, green and yellow-green.

SPLIT COMPLEMENTARY COLOUR SCHEMES
Split complementary colour schemes use any colour together with the two colours either side of its complementary colour.

TRIADIC COLOUR SCHEMES
A triadic colour scheme uses three evenly spaced colours. These could be the three primary colours, three secondary colours or three of the tertiary colours.

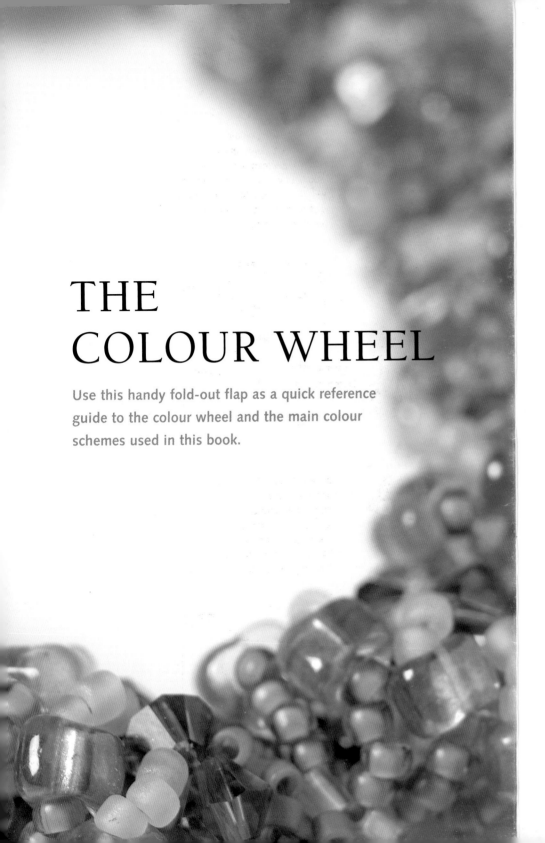

THE COLOUR WHEEL

Use this handy fold-out flap as a quick reference guide to the colour wheel and the main colour schemes used in this book.

Credits

Quarto would like to thank the artists for supplying work reproduced in this book. All artists are acknowledged in the captions beside their work.

Thank you to the project designers and makers:

Christine Bloxham: Analogous brooch; Warm-toned choker
Gill Hooper: Monochromatic earrings; Triadic spiral bracelet
Lindsay Kaubi: Woven bracelet
Sandra Wallace: Complementary colours; Tetradic necklace; Cool-toned lariat;
   Neutral necklace; Muted necklace.

All photographs and illustrations are the copyright of Quarto Publishing plc. While every effort has been made to credit contributors, Quarto would like to apologize should there have been any omissions or errors – and would be pleased to make the appropriate correction for future editions of the book.